THE POWER OF CH'I

LIVE LONGER
LOVE LONGER

THE POWER of CH'I
by GEOFF PIKE

The Secrets of Oriental Breathing for Health and Longevity

BELL PUBLISHING COMPANY

NEW YORK

Copyright © 1980 Illustrations and Text, Geoff Pike
All rights reserved.

This edition is published by Bell Publishing Company,
a division of Crown Publishers, Inc.,
by arrangement with Bay Books Pty. Ltd.
h g f e d c b a
BELL 1981 EDITION

Manufactured in the United States of America

Library of Congress Cataloging in Publication Data

Pike, Geoff, 1929-
   The power of Ch'i.

   1. Breathing exercises.   2. Health.   I. Title.
II. Title: Chi.
RA782.P44   1981   613'.912   81-6117
ISBN 0-517-34795-4   AACR2

To my wife, with thanks

"Because the eye gazes but can catch no
glimpse of it,
it is called elusive.
Because the ear listens but cannot hear it,
it is called rarefied.
Because the hand feels for it but cannot find it,
it is called the infinitesimal.
Its rising brings no light;
its sinking no darkness.
It is called Chi."

Tao Te Ching.

Acknowledgements

To my friends, Unicorn Wu,
Sifu Shakespeare Chan
and the instructors of
The Chin Wu Athletic Association of the
Philippines, for their patience and encouragement.

To Dean Rainer who, like all of
his kind, knows so much and
says so little.

Contents

Introduction

Five years ago, while living in the Philippines, I was found to have cancer. Today, at the age of fifty, I am fit, healthy and a great believer in the breathing exercises I have demonstrated in this book. I have no way of proving how much their daily practice had to do with my recovery but I do know that they have given me a new outlook and renewed vitality.

The shock of this news came at a time when I had reached a robust middle age and was enjoying the fruits of a successful career, an exciting if somewhat vagabond lifestyle and a tranquil marriage that gave me everything to live for. It caused me to look back at my life and wonder where, when, why and how I had first yielded to this awful disease. The inexplicable carcinoma that modern science seems powerless to fathom, this disorderly ganging up of cells, strikes a dread as great as any human or inhuman threat. Yet we live with it every day of our lives, ignoring its victims unless they are close to us and even avoiding the very word that describes it. There is nothing else to be done. It is something, we feel sure, that is set aside for others, never for us.

Perhaps it is this terrible feeling of loneliness, this helplessness of being singled out for the worst of all punishments, that makes one take stock. It is amazing how quickly a lifetime can shrink and how insignificant its purpose can become. One thing, however, that must shine through is the realisation that we alone are responsible for our bodies and their continued performance. Our care or neglect and our knowledge of our physical and mental make-up can do much to decide the state of health we enjoy or endure, especially in later years.

If you are to take any notice of this book and follow its suggestions at all, you should probably know something about its author and the life he has led. This is an outline of the life I was forced to look back on when threatened with the possibility of its untimely end.

I was born in Edmonton, London, in 1929. My early childhood was spent in Waltham Cross, Hertfordshire, where my father managed an off-licence liquor store. He was slowly dying as a result of too many months in the front-line trenches of Verdun and the Somme. Once he had been a gymnast and singer of note. Now, twenty years later, his lungs had all but collapsed and disease ran riot through his body and mind. I can remember the awful lassitude that took hold of him, a terrible, lonely anguish that left him less and less active. I was probably seven or eight years old when I vowed that such a thing would never be allowed to happen to me.

Circumstance then gave me a couple of enchanting years as an evacuee in the Essex countryside before I was admitted to a naval training ship. Harsh treatment, harsher food and hard work in bitter Welsh weather seemed to do me no harm, and by the time I went to sea at the age of fifteen and seven months, I had learned to smoke and drink like a man and was more than ready to grapple with the world.

My first great shock came on my sixteenth birthday. Stepping ashore in Kure, Japan, I took the train to Hiroshima. It was only a month or two after the atomic bomb had been dropped and what I saw and felt is still indescribable. Most astonishing of all was the sight of an old Japanese man standing among the ruins of what must have been his home and practising his breathing exercises.

I was to see more of this mysterious discipline in India and among the Chinese of Singapore and Indo-China. Each morning in the ports of Bombay and Calcutta there were those who would come down to the waterfront to exercise. It was in Saigon that I first saw a demonstration of the Chinese martial arts and the ancient breathing exercises that make its mastery possible.

After a year or so aboard an oil tanker in the Persian Gulf, I jumped ship in Sydney and went inland in search of trees. Trees are a thing you miss at sea. I drifted wherever opportunity took me. The outback of mid-western New South Wales showed me the inside of sheep station bunk houses, shearing sheds, railway fettlers' tents, saw mills and drovers' camps. The food was always rough but plentiful, work was hard and the drinking of beer in monumental quantities was an essential part of bush existence.

After two eventful and fascinating years, I was ready again for the smell of the sea and eventually found myself once more in England where I was conscripted into the Royal Artillery.

Demobbed in 1954, I returned to Australia, took a job in a warehouse and began studying art at night school. By 1960, I had become a respectable married man with all the accumulations of moderate success. My taste for plain and simple food was still with me, as was my capacity for beer and cigarettes. The need for physical work (for mine was the desk-bound job of a director of animated films) I fulfilled with half-hearted attempts at weight-training.

It was not until 1967 that I again came into contact with the Orient that had so impressed me as a boy. Now creative director of an advertising agency in Hong Kong, I used to walk each morning through Victoria Park or the villages of the New Territories and watch the Chinese of all ages and walks of life practising the same kinds of exercises I had seen twenty years earlier.

My interest grew and for the next six years, with the invaluable help of my Hong Kong-born wife, I travelled extensively in Southeast Asian countries to delve further into Oriental myth and legend, folklore and traditional attitudes towards health, healing and longevity.

In 1973, I felt I had seen enough of life and the world to be able to write about it in a manner that might interest others. With my wife's courageous consent, we took leave of career, home and friends to hibernate in the depths of Kent, Spain and the Philippines. With the assistance of a five-year Commonwealth Literary Fellowship this period produced a novel trilogy *Henry Golightly*, *Golightly Adrift* and *Golightly Outback* (Angus & Robertson/Pan Books), a novella, *To God From Hammersmith*, and this book, *The Power of Chi*.

Before We Begin

If your inner strength is matched only by your quietude of mind, then you are either too young to read this book, or this is not your particular mountain.

Are you one of those rare beings who consistently conducts a satisfactory life in good order and with reasonable success, effectively managing your mental and physical capabilities with sensible discipline? Have you learned with patience and foresight to nurture your health and treasure your one and only body with humility and gratitude?

Have you at all times avoided excess, never over-endulged your appetites and senses, maintained with fortitude and determination your precious youth, beginning each day with renewed zest and ending it in sound, untroubled sleep?

Is your sex life garlanded with sensual security, unhindered by inhibitions, haemorrhoids or hernia? Are you unaware and undisturbed by your joints, nerves, anxieties, the threats of war, pollution, disease, ageing, God Almighty and inevitable death?

Do your bowels move with the regularity of the rising and setting of the sun? Do you have a digestive system as dependable as the ebb and flow of the tide; does the temperature and rhythm of your blood waver only when it should; do the freedom of your movements, brightness of your eye and the bloom upon your skin bring glances of envy and admiration?

If you can say, yes, to all these conditions then you also probably do not need to read further. On the other hand, if you are an average specimen of twentieth century humanity, pronounced 'fit' by your general practitioner but knowing you could feel better, please read on.

It does not matter whether the realisation that you are 'not feeling as well as you should be', that you are 'not getting any younger' occurs to you in circumstances exotic or mundane. It could be under a guava tree on a Filipino hilltop as it was for me, in a Kyoto geisha house, behind a desk or a lawn mower, alone in bed or with someone else, running for the bus or just walking the dog. Neither does it matter what age you may be or the condition you are in. This book is not written for the middle-aged, but rather for those who feel middle-aged or know that some day they will.

What does matter is that we are all, without exception, emperor to eunuch, president to janitor, dependent upon one thing: this is the one and only essential available to all human beings in equal shares, to be used as we see fit. Breath gives life, sustains it and takes it away. Without it, we weaken, sicken and expire; because of it, we are revived, refreshed and quickly restored.

As with most things freely available and known to be good for us, we tend to take the important business of breathing for granted. The simple process of inhalation and exhalation need hardly be considered. Our supply of air is always constant and there is plenty of it. Only when it is threatened with pollution or infiltrated by unwelcome odours, do we become aware of it or indignant about our right to breathe it. Only when our breathing is impaired by age or ill health, do we show concern.

When we are fortunate enough to find ourselves on a mountain or close to the open sea, we fill our laboured lungs like nomads at an oasis, muttering things like 'absolute tonic . . . air like wine . . . feel it doing you good . . . glad to be alive'. And then, after a few hasty gulps, we return to our daily grind where the last thing we think of is deep breathing.

The Asians have known the importance of breath control for thousands of years. It is no coincidence that the great yogis and sadhus of India, the lamas of Tibet, the holy men and sages of China automatically took to mountainous regions for meditation and self-development or that all of their achievements, both physical and spiritual, began and ended with the harnessing of the air around them and its channelling into remarkable powers.

Unfortunately, access to mountain tops and the salty broads of oceans is becoming more and more restricted in the daily life of the average man. The promise of this book is to explain and demonstrate the truly amazing health benefits to be drawn from the air that surrounds you, whatever your location and whatever your circumstances.

What Is Chi?

What is this miraculous thing called Chi, this power that can rehabilitate failing health and recharge the human spirit, arrest illness and keep disease at bay? Can Chi really prolong vigorous life, regain lost years? Where did it come from? How can I find this key to the shining health, expanding energy and sheer physical joy I enjoyed briefly as a child. I had it then. Is it really possible that I can have it again? And, if I find it, how can I possibly hold onto it for the rest of my days?

To define Chi in simple terms one would have to know more than the yogis of India, the Tibetan lamas, the Shinto priests of Japan and the ancient sages of China. For at least five millennia wise men of the East have known its secret, but have been unable or unwilling to share it. The yogi calls it *Prana*, the lama calls it *Lung-gom*, to the follower of Shinto it is *Sakia-tundra* or *ki*, to the Chinese it is *Chi*. All seek the same source and all reach the same summit, as clear and immovable as a mountain on a diamond-bright day, as steady and changeless as that seat of meditation, the Himalayas. It is perhaps best described in the following passage from *The Secret of The Golden Flower: A Chinese Book of Life*. (trans. Richard Wilhelm, Harvest Books, New York, 1970).

'Heaven created water through the One. That is the true energy of the great One. If man attains the One he becomes alive; if he loses it he dies. But even if man lives in the energy (vital breath) he does not see the energy, just as fishes live in water but do not see the water. Man dies when he has not vital breath, just as fishes perish when deprived of water. If one guards this true energy, one can prolong the span of life and can apply the method of creating an immortal body.'

Two other well known students of the Eastern occult comment on the importance of breathing to longevity. Under the heading of 'Exercises for Prolonging Life', in *Chinese Folk Medicine* (Mentor Books, USA, 1974), Heinrich Wallnofer and Anna von Rottauscher state:

'Correct breathing is the basis of all exercises recommended in China for longevity, as well as for the cure of several diseases. As early as the fourth century BC, the philosopher Chuang-tzu promulgated that men of great wisdom fetch their breath from deep inside and below, while ordinary men breathe with the larynx alone. In other words, men were even then aware of the great value of deep respiration.

The principal purpose of Chinese gymnastic exercises, as is the purpose of the Indian yoga practices, is to attain proper circulation of the blood which, in turn, will ensure emotional balance and stability. This stability is to lend the body resistance against illnesses and consequently grant a longer life. Correct breathing is also mentioned very early as a means of cleansing the blood and body of their debris. Congestions may be removed and stiff joints limbered by adhering to the pertinent exercise instructions.

Contrary to many yoga practices, Chinese exercises are quite simple throughout and demand neither particular exertion, nor extraordinary and violent bodily contortions. Still, perseverance and strong willpower are indispensable if one wants to attain the final goal. All details are prescribed minutely, from the body posture to the exact position and motion of the fingers, and they have to be followed methodically.'

Surely, you say, such a blessing as Chi must be available to only a gifted few? On the contrary it is available to every man, woman and child, rich or poor, regardless of age, colour or creed. It is always there, awaiting those with the determination to reach for it. It surrounds us wherever we are. It is presented to us all at birth. We can use it as we please, cherish or waste it as we see fit. It is as close as our next breath or as distant as the horizon, the first gift given, the first lesson learned, and the last to be taken away.

I will never know how much the ancient exercises contained in this book had to do with my recovery from cancer: how much was due to super-voltage, my Maker, Chi, or a combination of all three. I am certain, though, that the continual daily practice of *The Eight Precious Sets of Exercises,* known to the Chinese as *Pa Tuan Tsin,* fortified me against the ravages of massive radiation and proved invaluable during recuperation. This opinion is shared by Dr Robert Morrison, Director of Radiation Therapy at Hammersmith Hospital in England.

Chi can be cultivated by learning the breathing exercises contained in this book, made available for the first time in the English language. It can be developed by practising them for a short period of time each day, in place of, or as well as, any exercise routine you may already have adopted. It costs nothing, requires no equipment or training partner . . . just air to breathe and room to move. You can acquire the power of Chi to whatever degree your patience and personal fortitude will allow and retain it for the rest of your life.

THE POWER of CH'I

PART ONE

FACING THE CONDITION YOU ARE IN

*'Rolled around in earth's diurnal course
with rocks and stones and trees'*
Wordsworth

The Hill

If you can believe the people you meet and talk to on the subject, or perhaps your own friends, whom you have watched as they grow older, it seems that middle age and the decline of physical condition creep up on some of us quite comfortably while others are hit as though with a club. The exceptions are usually very active individuals who either have the circumstances to allow a physically active lifestyle or a continuing dedication to some kind of sport.

We have all admired the professional ski instructor, swimming, tennis or football coach, the golf pro or gym instructor who is well past forty and still going strong. Consider a person who has spent a lifetime outdoors engaged in some kind of physical work. Chances are, he is stronger and sounder than his counterpart behind a desk, closeted in air-conditioning and artificial light. It stands to reason that the active outdoor type who uses his body continually stands a better chance of a long and healthy life than someone who thinks for a living and lets his body go to waste. In the mechanical 1980s, with physical effort becoming increasingly unpopular, it's not surprising that even something as obvious as this can become obscured by the daily round of surviving.

It is true that people in the West are becoming more aware of their responsibility for their own physical and mental welfare. There is less and less excuse for poor condition: we have increased leisure time, sporting and exercise facilities, gardens, swimming pools, home gymnasium equipment, diet charts, health foods, nature cures, vitamins and all the advice one can ask for in self-help books and mass media programmes. Many people take advantage of these opportunities and maintain a steady keep-fit routine throughout their lives but many others simply let themselves go and hope for the best.

For most of us the simple business of keeping body and soul in one piece, being responsible for a family, a home and a career is all we can cope with. We are 'kept going' by the sheer momentum of necessity, whether in a unionised work-force or on different levels of personal endeavour and ambition. It is often only in middle years, when vital energy begins to show a little wear, that it occurs to us that we may not be immortal. Our precious youth is all but spent because it probably has not been well maintained. Many of us have squandered it, taking fitness and health for granted and then wondering, quite suddenly, where it has gone. Is it too late to get it back? Health and strength came so naturally a few years ago . . . now it may take effort and discipline. We know it is worth it, but how?

The story that follows is how it happened for me — how I came to face the shape I was in and what I did about it. I have tried to give as accurate an account as possible and because this was undoubtedly the turning point of my life it is not difficult to remember.

The road to Taal Volcano wanders out from 'metro' Manila with the aimlessness of a lost buffalo and heads for the hills. It leaves the clutter of the outer barrios (slums), the carvers, the cane-makers, the Sari Sari stores selling salted eggs and pickled pig's ear, the countless urchins offering single cigarettes and single sticks of gum amid the tangle of traffic. It straightens out between the rice paddies that flow, as if infinite, towards Batangas and the Sibuyan Sea.

The landscape becomes prettier as you climb higher: sugar cane, pineapple and coconut groves. Villages are few and far between: clean, earth yards well swept, fences made of wartime landing strip and painted white, bougainvillaea and wild banana shading grass thatch. Dusty chickens and muddy pigs scatter as you drive through. The people grin. As in most countries, they get happier and friendlier the further you get from the city. I was travelling in the company's air-conditioned, chauffeur-driven Chevrolet to a seminar at Taal. The company thought the mist-shrouded majesty of the volcano and its sapphire lake was a suitable background for the business at hand and therefore worth the two-and-a-half hour drive. I was an hour out when the front offside tyre blew, right in the middle of nowhere.

It was a hot day. It was hot all over. The earth was hot, the grass, the trees, the bushes, stones, sprouts, shoots, everything was hot. Even the birds hid among toasted leaves. Everything that stood, grew, flew or just lay around and burned was oppressed by the heat. Consumed by it. I was hottest of all. I wondered if I would have felt as afflicted by it had I been ten years younger. I tried to remember. I couldn't. I was too damn hot to think.

Maybe that was why I decided to climb the hill. It could be cooler up there. It wasn't! A single guava tree sheltered its peak like a peasant's hat. Its shade was sauna-hot. I looked down to where the car baked, a silver shell in the smothering shade of bamboo that cracked like stones in a fire and rustled dead skin leaves under the shrilling weight of cicadas.

That car was something special. The kind we all watched going by when we were on the way up and dreamed of owning when we made it to where we were going. Right now, it looked about as impressive as the tin can I used to kick down gutters. The jacket I carried was pretty special too. Tropical fabric, carefully chosen from an expensive wad of muted shades, in the best available taste. Hand-cut, styled and stitched by costly craftsman's fingers, just for me. Up here, it felt like a wet sugar sack.

I should have felt great in that great suit, looking back at that great car. I didn't. I felt sick. I felt strung out. I felt like an old man in a young man's pants. Insects whirred and clacked in the leaves over my aching skull. The cool green skin of a guava fruit showed, just out of reach. Did you know the inside of a guava stays cool like a melon, even in this equatorial intensity? I tried for one. Stretched and made an attempt to jump. It was like reaching for the hand of God. Sweat, not perspiration. Plain, salty sweat ran down the inside of that special suit the way rain runs down a roof in a monsoon. The only heart I'll ever own beat like a Salvation Army drum on a sunny Sabbath. Blood churned around, a mill-race in my ears. A heart attack? After taking on one lousy little hill?

Knees of guava jelly. I sat. The rock was hot, so I stood. A short pull at the silver hip flask, encased in Spanish leather and monogrammed in gold. The best of Scottish malt to the rescue. The cigarette I lit, selected from a flat gold case, was the brand of smoke expected of successful executives, to be lit with a gold Dunhill. Sucking back the smoke and looking at my solid gold watch. You know the kind of watch it was? Right! A Rolex. Hewn from a solid ingot, the ad said. I had it all. Man, was I successful! But I couldn't reach a guava, or climb a tree to save my sensational life!

So there I am. Reviewing my life from the top of this piddling hill. Have you ever done that? Not necessarily from a Filipino hilltop, maybe from your office window, or at the golf club after a less than spectacular performance. On the beach, maybe, holding your stomach in till your ears ring. After an unsuccessful sexual encounter. In the bath with everything out of sight but a belly-button full of suds. At the bedroom mirror with muscles flexed and nothing showing but your blood pressure. A popular place for quiet analysis is the sanctuary of the bathroom, wondering why things don't work the way they used to. It's a great place to come to terms with your hair, teeth, testicles and overall plumbing.

Anyway, right now, back to me, and my unattainable guava. I was pretty successful in business. Not a tycoon or anything like that, but pretty well set-up in a self-made, independent sort of way. The company car, the driver, the wardrobe, the heavy trinkets, the five-star hotels, monumental menus, fat expense account and first-class air fares all went along with fat fees. Mine was a pretty sought-after existence. A consultant in the world-wide business of 'Creative Communications'.

Usually, it's called advertising. But when you've been at it as long as I have, you like to think of it as communication. That's when you've sold just about all there is to sell, from peanuts to computers, to just about all the people there are in our share of the world and somebody else's share; sold soft drinks where they need water, and candy where they need medicine; and learned about likes and dislikes, market reactions and motivations. When you have used the Big Brother tactics of market research and consumer analysis to manipulate minds with purchase propositions, persuasion, penetration, test targets and creative strategies, then you like to think of it as communication. But really, it is advertising. What we do for a living doesn't matter either. We're getting older every day. Maybe more or less successful, but older. What are we doing about it? That's what matters!

So, that was my particular concern around the time I realised I was becoming a physical failure. I had reached the top of my professional tree. Trouble-shooting for international advertising agencies over half the world, in particular the Oriental half, but I could have been washing cars in Baltimore or seeding salmon in the Scottish Highlands. It wouldn't have made any difference. I had used up the first half of my life. I had squandered it like a pirate digging into a chest of silver. I was looking at the bottom. Where had it all gone? I try and think back over the scattered years, to when I could have raced down that hill and up again without breathing hard.

Youth. I remember mine. It probably wasn't anything at all like yours.

Then again, maybe it was in some ways. For one thing, we both took it for granted. Because we never ached or strained or sprained. Middle age was something that happened to other people, like getting hit by a bus. We were immortal. Remember? Age was always five years ahead of us, bellies and bald heads eons away. Impotency, or rather the sad result of prolonged trial by tension, as remote from instant erections as false teeth.

Midday. Hairs on my wrist stuck flat and moisture under the glass of the fabulous Rolex Oyster. I was going to be late. I wondered if my driver felt this blast furnace, black as a beetle around that wounded front wheel. Filipinos never move fast. This one was no exception. He was thin in the gut and thick in the head. Muscles, well-defined, under that uniform shirt he'd shed, rolled with his efforts the way mine once rolled.

Some Simple Tests

'It is a duty to be healthy.' Old yogi saying.

So that's how it happened for me. Of course, these little moments of truth pass and we feel 'quite alright' again. We bury them quickly. We may be so unaccustomed to exercise that our make-up soon settles down to its indolent routine and we get along perfectly well, until the next time. And there will be a next time unless, of course, we eventually fall ill or have an accident from which an unfit body cannot recover. You don't have to climb a hill without a hat in 100 degrees and 100 per cent humidity to feel like dropping out of the big parade. You can let your guard down, lower your defences, get a little afraid, a little tired of it all anytime and anywhere. But sooner or later, it will happen. So don't wait. If you want to get some idea of the kind of shape you are in there are a couple of very simple tests you can try right now, in the office, the kitchen, the bathroom, the garden, anywhere but a phone booth. All you need is room enough to breathe, spread your arms, jump 15 cm and bend double.

First the lungs. Try taking three very long, deep breaths, inhaling through the nose as slowly and silently as you can. Hold each breath for the count of three, exhale through the mouth as slowly and silently as you can and again count to three before taking the next breath. It is likely that you'll find the inhalation shortish and somehow unsatisfactory, like only finding the capacity to drink half a glass of water when you're thirsty. You may find the exhalation hard to control, as though your lungs are unaccustomed to overfilling and eager to spill out.

Average lungs don't like to be reminded that they are only working at half their capacity, even if they feel overworked. You may experience brief dizziness, possibly fleeting patterns before your eyes. You will almost certainly feel strange in some way if you really tried to fill your normally half-filled lungs, especially if you are a smoker.

Before considering concentrated breathing of any kind, it is vitally important to 'build up to it'. The fact that you have been breathing all your life doesn't immediately qualify you for intense breathing exercises. Look at it this way: you have been walking all your life, but you would soon drop out of a marathon; you have been lifting things all your life, but you would be unwise to attempt lifting a 100 kg weight; you may have been swimming since you were a child, but could you swim 8 km to shore?

Most 'normal' breathers would find it distinctly uncomfortable, even painful to suddenly begin filling their lungs to four or five times their usual capacity. Your system just isn't used to taking in that much oxygen at once. Fuel of life or not, you can overfill your tank too suddenly. The trick is to clean it out and make it larger for a start. Unless you are already well practised in deep breathing, the best thing you can do is to set this book aside when you have read it, for a week or a month or whatever it takes to build up your lung power.

Begin practising deep breathing whenever and wherever it occurs to you to do so. While walking, resting, working or even preparing for sleep. Make regular, conscious efforts to increase your breath load. During this process your ribcage will expand and with it, the ease and capacity of your respiration. You may find that you gain up to 2 cm around the chest. In a month's time, it may have expanded another 2 cm or even more to the full extent your frame will allow. In the first six months of conscious breathing my own chest expansion went from 97 cm to 105 cm to 113 cm; in the second six months from 113 cm to 116 cm to 120 cm.

Now that you have found that your breathing techniques could use a little attention, let's get to the flexibility of waist, neck, arms and legs. If you're in normal health and over thirty, that is to say, you don't plough fields, chop trees, demolish buildings or re-sleeper railway lines for a living, you have probably lost your stomach muscles or they are well on the way out. Once abdominal muscles have been allowed to break down they are very difficult to rebuild. It is comparatively easy though, to firm up and strengthen the whole belly region or mid-section.

The simplest and most foolproof test for waist and back condition is as follows.

Stand erect with heels together. Inhale deeply and slowly, keeping the knees locked and legs rigid. Bend slowly forward, exhaling gently through the mouth as you do so and try touching your toes. Force your fingertips as close to the floor as you can, if they easily reach, spread them or try touching it with your knuckles or palms.

At the end of your maximum bend, you should be empty of breath. Count silently to three and straighten, slowly inhaling a fresh breath through the nose on your way up. Repeat this three times. The ease with which you reach the floor will tell you how much work needs to be done on your middle. Remember, an outsize waistline or a stiff back is never irretrievable and although you may not again see those neatly defined rows of hard muscle rippling above your swim trunks, you'll fortify what you've got there and lose a lot of excess weight in the process.

If you are in fairly normal condition and you do these bends properly, the tendons in the back of your legs, particularly behind the knees, will feel ready to snap like over-stretched guitar strings. Don't worry, they won't. Your legs may feel a little shaky, knees a little weak and your breathing may not be as gentle as the sighing of a breeze through pines. This only proves how much you need the exercise. Even if you find you can hardly reach your shins, within six weeks of practice the leg-stretching and waist-bending in Pa Tuan Tsin will have you pressing your open palms flat on the floor and touching your knee with you nose with the ease of a ballet dancer.

There are other simple tests for flexibility of neck, legs and arms that you can try on the spot. First the neck: stand erect, rise on your toes and slowly try looking behind you without swivelling your shoulders. Try this three times to the left and three times to the right. You'll probably find you can't get far without risk of breaking something. After six weeks of Pa Tuan Tsin, you will think you are made of India rubber.

Next, the legs. Stand erect, with heels together. Inhale deeply and slowly. Lower your body gradually, exhaling as you go down until you are squatting in a deep knee bend. Do not touch the floor with your fingers, count to three and try slowly standing up. If you can do this three times without drums beating in your ears and your kneecaps going off like toy pistols, try another three. Probably, you will find it hard to rise steadily on the first attempt: almost impossible on the second and barely make it on the third. After six weeks of Pa Tuan Tsin you will be bobbing up and down as easily as a well-greased, fiddler's elbow.

Lastly, the arms and shoulders. Stretch them out to their full extent, locking the elbows and force them back at shoulder level. See how far behind you can reach without threat of dislocation or springing a rib. Ignore the cracking noises and you'll probably gain a centimetre or two. In six weeks of Pa Tuan Tsin you will have gained 60 cm, smooth as a swallow in flight.

If all this sounds strenuous, and if you are out of condition it no doubt is, remember that you have not just completed a course of difficult isotonic exercise. All you have done is touch your toes, a deep knee bend, turned your head and spread your arms properly . . . all perfectly natural movements that hardly call for therapeutic instruction or medical supervision.

As we were saying, these little twinges of concern or even guilt which arise when we realise we are not giving our bodies a reasonable chance of carrying us through a long and lively lifetime, pass as quickly as they crop up. Lethargy, refusal to face the facts or just being too busy to do anything about it are the reactions that usually smother sudden bouts of determination. Another junk lunch, another drink and another smoke will make it go away. It's so much easier to convince yourself that you don't really feel that bad. In fact, most of the time, you feel pretty damn good. Except when you put yourself to a simple test or two such as those I have suggested.

In my case that climb to the hilltop with all its palpitations, was the crunch. It didn't pass. Not this time. I knew it never would unless I did something about it. I'd finally been hit by that bus and unless I got up, it was going to run right over me and back again. Then, as is so often the case in important stages of life, fate, destiny, God or just plain luck, took a hand. I met a man who impressed me with his being, changed my attitudes towards life and health with his example and pointed me in the right direction.

PART TWO

THERE IS NO SUCCESS WITHOUT HEALTH

'Disease, dullness, indecision, carelessness,
sloth, worldliness, mistaken views, losing
the way and instability — these splurgings
of the mind are obstacles that co-exist
with disordered inbreathing and outbreathing.'
Patanjali

Enter Mr Wu

I was at a meeting the day after the blow-out on the Batangas road. Some smart young account director was on his well-shod feet, flashing cufflinks and research findings at a row of grim-faced money-men. I wasn't listening.

Later, after the meeting and at the sumptuous hotel lunch I'd become so accustomed to, it was still on my mind. My health was on the way out and with it, my confidence. It was over the coffee and cognac that I decided to do something about it. I refused a cigar and a re-fill. It was a start. I had already bought my tracksuit and running shoes when into my life came Mr Wu. It is important that you share my first impressions of him and the way our relationship developed and why.

He had not attended the morning's session or the sumptuous luncheon. Mr Wu was a new addition to the agency's list of impressive clients. The securing of his business, in which I had played a major hand, caused great excitement. He was known simply as Mr Wu and his executives, the usual shifty, insecure bunch of yes-men, spoke of him in whispers, either through reverence or fear.

He arrived at the afternoon meeting, punctually. Unusual for a very rich Chinese. As the company rose like the fourth form greeting their headmaster, he moved swiftly to his chair at the head of the table, issued a brief but a pleasant smile and a nod and sat down. Dispensing with the usual insincere handshakes and meaningless introductions, he poured himself a glass of water and by his very bearing indicated that the presentation should begin.

I had been flown across the world to show this man how to make more money, and to prepare my recommendations I had been given access to the archives of his company. It was not the usual assignment. His company had an unusual history, and Mr Wu was a most unusual man. He was extremely rich. Beyond speculation, it was said. A Fukien Chinese who had started life as the son of a penniless woodsman in the hills of Shantung on mainland China. It was there, the story went, that he discovered the secret of ginseng (the elixir of life) and other powerful and mysterious herbs and preparations that to the Western world represent Chinese medicine.

Now he owned a chain of stores throughout Southeast Asia, his warehouses supplied exclusively from Red China. From this had grown, among other businesses, one of the largest and most successful export companies in Asia. It was this vast enterprise that he now wished to develop and diversify into European and American markets. It was my job to advise him.

In the delicate business of bringing together buyer and seller from two totally different worlds, it has always been one of my opening tactics to make a thorough study of the personality I am being paid to impress and convince. This had not been possible with Mr Wu. I had been carefully, almost fearfully briefed by his top executive. The president, it appeared, was still far more enamoured with the earthier aspects of his herbal empire than the dalliances of the board room. His business had grown through knowledge of his product, the Chinese brilliance in business and not a little luck, timing, risk and confidence in himself and his destiny. He was far more likely, I was told, to be found chatting and taking tea in a back street Chinatown store or off on a field trip to Canton, than enthroned in an air-conditioned office or conference room.

I watched him closely during preliminary niceties, which he suffered in polite discomfort. He was a quiet man, with the neat, medium build of most northern Chinese, but appeared particularly well-knit and lithe under the sombre, perfectly-tailored business suit. He scarcely spoke and was hard put to conceal impatience, but he radiated an awe-inspiring sense of power. The aura of sheer energy seemed to surround him like a force. Not one of his subordinates spoke unless he addressed them with a glance or a question. Their eyes, slippery with caution, seldom left his face. No one smoked, a blessing in that badly-ventilated tomb of a room, with its mock leather chairs, projection screen and ancient air-conditioners bumbling along like muted bus engines. Mr Wu did not approve of smoking. He had requested that no-one smoke and that only water or Chinese tea be served instead of the usual overdose of instant coffee and fancy biscuits.

He listened with growing intolerance to the stammered strategies and rehearsed recommendations on how he should spend a half million dollars on the infiltration of foreign markets. If he was impressed or disgusted, pleased or disappointed, it was impossible to say. Only by the slight movement of his head, the sudden, piercing challenge of his eye and a rare change of expression could his understanding or approval be gauged.

He was by no means a domineering man. On the contrary, his presence had a strangely calming effect upon what usually becomes a clamorous conflict for self-justification and puerile pettiness. He seemed to fill dynamically his place at the head of the table, almost appearing to oscillate power-waves at will. His English was measured but nearly perfect, his words precise and lyrical in the old Chinese way. His gaze was fixed unflinchingly upon his subject until bored. His reactions transmitted little currents up and down the polished slab of acacia that served as a board table.

I had sat at many such meetings throughout the money centres of Asia during the past decade, many of them attended and conducted by taipans of this man's magnitude. Mysterious men who maintained a wolfish control of business throughout most of the region. Never had I been as impressed or affected as I was by the presence of Mr Wu.

The campaign I had devised for the Sun Moon Export Company was simple, directly and accurately aimed at its target without frills or flounces. It was the kind of communication I felt certain Mr Wu would understand and accept. I was right. His nods were frequent and, at appropriate points in the presentation, I was rewarded with the rarity of a smile. From him, it was an accolade. Nerves were a condition I had conquered long before, yet for the opening moments, pinned by those unshifting eyes, I felt my bowels weaken at the thought of failure.

Another trick I had learned in ten years of Asian advertising was to do my homework thoroughly, to make an in-depth study of the product I was to sell and the consumer considered most likely to go out and buy it. I had spent a week closeted in my hotel room with every book I could find on Chinese medicine and herbal remedies. As it happened I had been a keen collector of Taoist poetry and I had found a place in the campaign to quote a piece which I felt symbolised the effects of a particular tranquillising mixture. It goes like this:

'Bamboo shadows sweep the stairs,
but the dust is undisturbed.
The moonlight penetrates deep into the pond,
but leaves no trace in the water.

The wind ceases, yet blossoms continue to fall.
Birds sing, yet the valley becomes quieter.
In the bamboo groves, my thatched house is built by rocks.

Through openings among stems of the bamboo,
the distant village is seen.
I take it easy all day, and receive no visitors,
but the pure breeze sweeps a path leading to my door.'

It worked. His parting words were a gift, 'For a man who is not Chinese, you have great perception.'

It was some weeks later, when the execution of the campaign had been completed, approved and scheduled that the real honour came. A stiff square envelope containing his personal notepaper and a freely scrawled invitation to visit his home during the weekend.

He was swimming when I arrived. Long casual strokes up and down the turquoise length of his pool with the leisurely grace of an otter. I was not offered alcohol but the cold juice of calamansi, the little round lime of the Philippines, and a dish of pickled quail eggs.

He completed several laps while I sat in comfortable cane and admired the rare golden coconut palms that shaded the pool. A profusion of flowers invaded the high walls of his garden in the costly privacy of Makati's Millionaire Village. Bougainvillaea of every colour battled for prominence and the uncut lawns were scattered thickly with the perfumed heads of frangipani. Hibiscus blooms as big as dinner dishes spread in pink, white, scarlet and deep apricot.

His servants were male, graciously efficient in the way I imagined of old China, their black-slippered feet silent as bare soles on the sawn stone flagging of the patio. It was a surprise. Female servants, the dark-skinned, large-eyed Filipinas from the provinces were an expected accessory to the house of a rich Chinese. Simple, devoted and easily intimidated.

He saw me eying the uncut grass as he hoisted himself effortlessly from the pool and accepted a towel. He had sensed my surprise although I had not shown it.

'I see I disappoint you.' He dabbed water from his creamy skin. 'The

Hainanese male makes the best servant. He knows what he would expect for himself. He makes the world's best masseur and one can move freely without inhibition.'

It was the first time I had heard him laugh.

'Without lapses of the head and heart each month of the year, as it is with females.' Handing over the towel for a light silk robe.

'For me, sex is like fine food. To be exquisitely prepared, expertly served and tantalising to the taste; taken only when necessary and then savoured slowly and in many courses.' He accepted a glass of juice and the servant left. 'I prefer not to be surrounded by food. One could become a glutton.'

There had been time to see his body before he covered it. Finely balanced, hairless and smooth as a woman's, the contours of a dancer. Across the conference room, stiff and unbending in the dark suit, I had taken him to be in his well-preserved fifties. Now, moving as he did with great flexibility, his physique seemed that of a much younger man.

'As for the grass, I do not like to make things bleed unnecessarily.'

During the course of an intriguing afternoon I discovered two fascinating things about Mr Wu. Firstly, that he had been a keen student of the Chinese martial art of *Wu Shu* (wrongly thought of as *Kung Fu*) since his early childhood in the forests of China. And secondly, the astonishing fact that he was almost seventy years old.

'Yours was the fifth such presentation I have listened to in past weeks. Most of them made me despair. You are the first who has taken the trouble to try and understand your subject.'

I waited. It was not enough. This, after all, was my business.

'I do not believe in advertising,' he continued, 'the goods I trade in are nature's gift. They do not need to be sold like soap and cigarettes. They sell themselves. I have never before considered it but my advisers say that I must. I leave such things to them.' He sipped, pausing just long enough to do so. 'I think your work will introduce my products to the West in a manner of which I will approve. Your approach is sensitive, even artistic. It is worthy of my confidence and I thank you for it.'

It was still not enough.

'It is not the money that will be made,' he smiled. 'Not entirely. There are many health secrets that were used in China when your people lived in caves. It is time they were shared.' Again the smile. 'If they also make me richer . . .' he raised his hands in submission.

'There is one thing more. Something I can do for you in return. I was trained in my profession by a great Master, my father. He taught me many mysterious things, among them the ability to read a man's inner condition by the colours of his aura.* Yours are not good. If you wish, I will help you. But you must be patient, very patient. And you must believe in yourself.'

There the conversation had ended.

---

* *It is true that each of us is surrounded by a field of force. It is also claimed by those considered to be psychic in Western society, that the 'aura' of a person is often clearly visible to them in rainbow colours of varying strengths. The old-style Chinese medical practitioner learned to 'read' these colours in order to diagnose bodily disorders and conditions before touching the patient.*

Mr Wu's acceptance of me over a considerable period and many lengthy discussions opened doors that until then had been closed to non-Chinese. I saw him many times after that first hot Manila afternoon of calamansi juice, quiet conversation and pickled quail eggs. Once I had overcome the faint uneasiness I always feel around men who do not seem to like women, there were quiet dinners, sometimes at his home, but usually in the private rooms of Chinatown's back-street restaurants. He introduced me to the rigorous scaldings and scourings of the true Shanghai bath. Again, we were attended only by males, powerful Shanghainese whose fingers took you apart piece by piece and put you back together again, ready for the road.

Just when I was beginning to think he was impotent, celibate or homosexual he took me to a special house. The girls were young, pure Chinese. We were received as honoured guests and over jasmine tea, he told me of three wives and an astounding number of children, grandchildren and great-grandchildren. This, he explained, was where he came when it was time for pleasure. It was seldom he admitted, often one hundred days would elapse before his next visit. His Chi, he explained, was far too precious to be wasted. We left after a glass of jasmine tea and he made no further effort to prove his status. I am sure the brief visit was intended to put me at ease.

Our discussions were almost always a balance of tension and relaxation, humility and ego, gentleness and aggression, tolerance and impatience, turbulence and quietude, resulting in the question of defence and attack. I was his pupil more than his friend. He probed first my outer ego, my reactions to violence, my opinion of myself, my attitude to others. With patience and always politeness, he reached into places and feelings I had not considered for years. I think he dug up what remained of my soul. I was not always aware of being tested, as well as instructed.

His philosophy of life, ambition and attainment was clear-cut: without absolute health, there was nothing worth having. And to him, the discovery, understanding, development and preservation of Chi was the keystone around which all else was built. To attain Chi was like building a new foundation to replace or renew support of one that had become weakened by time and its ravages. On either side of Chi, holding the keystone firmly in place, there must be two things, patience and discipline. Patience above all with yourself, your own body and its limitations.

Patience breeds discipline, discipline breeds fortitude, fortitude conquers uncertainty and replaces it with confidence. From this well-spring of confidence that can be tapped in every human spirit flows the river of physical and mental well-being. This, he assured me in all seriousness, was that which had been sought since time immemorial as the fountain of youth. He talked of holy men who reached beyond the physical to the spiritual: Indian gurus prolonging their existence into well over one hundred and sometimes two hundred years in the rarefied air of the Himalayas, mountain peasants of Russia and Mongolia, great sages of China, lamas of Tibet, Buddhist monks of Thailand and throughout South-east Asia, bomos of Malaysia and Indonesia, Shinto priests of Japan and the ancient order of samurai. All of them sought long life in which age brought strength and power rather than weakness and decay. All were men of the East and all, he pointed out, practised and mastered the art of breath control. As if to demonstrate the fact or perhaps

explain it, he gave me the following poem:

> When the mind is detached, the place is quiet.
> I gather chrysanthemums under the eastern hedgerow
> And silently gaze at the southern mountains.
> The mountain air is beautiful in the sunset.
> I drink of it as from a snow-fed stream.
> It purifies me, it strengthens me, it calms me.
> It becomes a river within me.
> Its tributaries refresh and renew sinew, bone and marrow.
> It is one with my blood.
> In time it becomes a torrent
> To be summoned up as a storm upon the mountain.
> This torrent is the fuel of life.
> It is called by the masters, Chi

Such thoughts and discussions, very briefly summarised, formed the basis of Mr Wu's philosophy. All that is to follow came from knowing him.

The Brotherhood

The address on the envelope Mr Wu gave me led to a disused office block on the Chinatown waterfront. This is the old part of Manila, known as the Escolta, in the heart of the downtown business area. Once the scene of bitter fighting between Chinese and Filipino and still entered with a certain amount of caution by non-Chinese, it is the classic Hollywood film location. Entering the towering Friendship Gate with its rampant dragons, I felt about as welcome as a bishop in a brothel.

Tug boats, barges, bum-boats and scows of every length, beam, tonnage and state of repair bumped about on the khaki currents of the Pasig River. It was hard to see where the river stopped and the town began. Scavengers' huts squatted on its banks in a patchwork of stolen lumber and flattened oil drums, observation posts for the streams of flotsam that swirled in the wakes of passing river craft. The squatters gave way to cars, the cars to concrete. Noodle shops, tea shops, beauty and barber shops cohabited with sheet metal workers, tinsmiths, mechanics, hardware and the daytime dungeons of the night-time bars.

I moved with the tide of people. Five Chinese to every Filipino, flooding the narrow streets in conflicting eddies and whirlpools. The ever-building, ever-adding overflow of Chinatown, a commotion of metal on metal, wood on wood, the revving of engines, the clatter of horse-drawn calasas, a whiff of old Spain in the den of the Oriental, the tumult of dialect, the stench of heat and humanity.

A blind bootblack guarded the unswept stairs I was searching for. Beside him, the buckled cage of an antique lift crouched among its intricacies of iron trellis and ungreased cables. I decided to take the stairs. Past smells of boiling noodles and frying fat, one barred and unused door after another, welded fast with grime. I mount empty floor after empty floor.

From above, perhaps two floors up, come sounds. The soft thump of muffled footfalls striking old floorboards, advancing and retreating to a rhythmic chant, stopping and starting to barked commands. I decide to pause and gather myself. Five flights had me out of breath. It wouldn't do to present

Mr Wu's letter of introduction with unsteady hand or answer questions with a gasp and a wheeze.

I sat on the stair to consider and felt strangely alone. Suspended between those deserted, rat-ridden rafters, echoing with age, was I right to be here? I had seldom in my lifetime felt so uncertain of my surroundings, so lost and so unimportant, never so unsuited to a time or place. I could turn back and save making a fool of myself. Back to the club with its airy bar under the cooling ceiling fans. Nothing to contend with but a procession of ice-cold San Miguels, the ladies frolicking in the pool and the activity of the tennis court. I could sit at the bar watching someone else put in all the effort. I almost convinced myself all this discipline and patience was alright for fanatics like Wu. He was born to it; such effort was suited to his beliefs. He was cut out for its demands, it was part of his blood, bone and marrow. Did I really want to go on?

I thought of the chaps at the club. Chaps like me, who ate and drank far too much and exercised too little. Most of them were expatriates or regular travellers. Life in the East was often a trap for them. There were those that couldn't leave because they did their business there and those that couldn't stay away because the place and the people they returned to were pale by comparison. There is often glamour in places where you are not really meant to be and boredom where you belong. But there was boredom here, too, once you become blasé about instant sex, the massage parlours with their executive treatments, the night spots, hotel bars and downtown dives.

The sounds from above brought me back. The stair was hard. There were cobwebs in the grill of the lift well.

'It will not be necessary for me to accompany you. Master C. is an old friend. This letter is all you will need to give him. I think he will accept you on my judgement.' Mr Wu had given me the letter a week or two before, the evening before leaving on an extended trip to China. 'You must make up your own mind if you are to use it. I can only direct you to the foot of the mountain, I cannot make you climb.'

His genuine interest in my health had been something that had seemed to evolve quite naturally from our casual acquaintance. The day had come when he had shown his concern after a vigorous game of pelota, a sort of Filipino version of squash played with a short-handled racket. I was badly out of breath and had shown it. He had observed my state with a slight frown of concern.

Later, he had put me to some basic tests. Tests, he admitted mildly, that would not be recognised by Western doctors. They were, in fact, outlawed in the British colony of Hong Kong, even though they were a thousand years older than any European method of diagnosis. No, he was not a doctor, he allowed, but in his life-time study of herbalism and practice of Wu Shu he had learned to recognise most of the things likely to go wrong with a man. He had seen irregularities in my aura, he explained. I was not to be alarmed, the aura of most Western men he bothered to observe showed a lack of knowledge of their own bodies.

'There is nothing seriously wrong with you,' he had announced with satisfaction on finishing his tests, all of which had begun and ended with the lightest touching of various parts of my body. 'I have been reading your silent pulse. You have two, you know. The silent one is the one that tells everything.'

I was overweight, he said solemnly, my wind was blown, joints stiff, sinews taut, muscles soft, circulation sluggish, blood pressure erratic, respiration at half speed, liver enlarged, kidneys coping inadequately, spleen and bladder weakening and extended, heart overloaded and underpowered, and lungs working at half capacity. None of which was doing my nerves any good. I was, he assured me gently, a typical Western specimen of middle-aged man. He laughed aloud at my reaction.

'Of course I exaggerate, but not so much. All of these things will befall you in the next five to ten years unless they are prevented now. It is never too late.'

His decision to send me to Chin Wu had seemed a casual one. Now I realised it was not. I had been under observation for many months. 'I cannot be sure that you will be accepted. You are non-Chinese.' He laughed. 'You would be the only foreign devil in the class.'

Mr Wu had been checking the contents of his briefcase before leaving for the airport. 'I believe that what you may learn you will put to good use. I do not say they can make a boy of you, but they can make you feel like one.'

We shook hands. 'It is now up to you.' Then he was gone.

The Chinese who took the letter from me was of medium height, weight and build, with a pleasant but expressionless face. He was too polite to show surprise at being confronted by a foreigner. He asked me to sit while he read the letter, which was unexpectedly long. Several pages in Mr Wu's neat hand. While he read, I looked around the cubicle of an office, its walls lined with photographs of martial artists in action, ancient drawings and documents, silk banners embroidered with Chinese characters. Distant street sounds filtered up through slanted open windows.

In the gym itself, I could see perhaps twenty men. Mainly Chinese, with a sprinkling of Filipinos, they were practising ballet-like movements upon the long, wide stretch of empty floorspace. They wore loose-fitting, baggy pants, the traditional black canvas Chinese slippers and the scarlet sash of Chin Wu. Sandbags and punching blocks hung from the roof beams and an intriguing array of ancient weaponry flanked the walls: tridents, lances, spears, staves, leather armour and swords of all shapes, neatly racked.

There was a surprising lack of the effort, sweat and sound usually found in a gym. Instead, the padded footfalls were accompanied by the pervading scent of sandalwood. A spray of joss sticks flowered from a brass incense burner before a shrine which guarded the entrance to the training space.

In the five minutes that followed, I watched astounding feats of sheer, unbelievable power. I saw speed and grace combined in a way I had never imagined. Leaps of two to two and a half metres from a standing position. Kicks that packed the power of pile-drivers at impossible angles and heights, while others gently performed the ballet-like movements of Tai Chi.

During my years in Asia, I had followed the martial arts as a keen and envious spectator. I had watched bouts of Tai Kwon Do in Korea; Kendo, Sumo and Aikido in Japan; Karate in Hong Kong and Singapore; Arnis in

the Philippines. Once, as far back as 1945, I had witnessed an old and
feeble-looking man in Saigon defeat all comers aboard an allied troopship:
United States marines, British commandos, Australian diggers. He had invited
them all to challenge him. One, two, three or even four at a time. They
had tried for an hour but not one could lay a hand on him. He had picked
up the stakes, bowed politely, and moved on to the next ship.

The memory of the old man had stayed with me for a quarter of a century,
and now, in this barren square on top of an abandoned office block in Manila's
Chinatown, I knew I was looking at the source of his power. I was observing
the training methods of the authentic art of Wu Shu.

The sound of a striking match made me turn. The Chinese had crumpled
the letter into a ball. He set a match to it and when it had caught, let
it drop into the incense burner.

'I have read the letter from brother Wu. We will think about it. You
must come back in one week.'

I passed the blind bootblack seven times in seven weeks before I was accepted
by Chin Wu. At each visit, I was courteously asked the same questions, by
different instructors.

Why did I wish to learn? Was it for self-defence? Was it for health alone
that I sought to develop Chi? How did I respond to violence, to insult, to
indignity and injustice? Could I stand pain? Would I conceive of killing?
Yes, they knew what had been written in the letter from brother Wu. They
must hear it from me and judge for themselves. They must be sure. My
answers were always the same: I was interested in the health aspects only,
I would defend but never attack, in order to be gentle one must be strong
(quoting Mr Wu). On the eighth visit, I was admitted. I had passed the
test of patience and proved my interest by returning eight times without
a sign of protest.

The Oath

It was dark by the time they were ready for me. Outside, the noise of
Chinatown had changed its tone for the night. Leisure sounds, traditional
Oriental music sing-songed out from tea shops and restaurants. From the
bars, juke boxes peddled the latest Western hits, the clamour of the day's
business had slowed down to the brightly lit bustle of evening. Neon, late
shops, the flames from curbside stoves and over the river shadows with an
occasional glimpse of lamps and pitch flares, the Friendship Gate flood-lit
in scarlet, as richly strung with coloured lights as a fairground carousel. The
last of the students had dressed and gone. I waited. Watching the calasas
pass each other on Jones Bridge, polished brass side lights burning tiny, orange
oil flames. They mixed like sparks with the street lamps. Master C. appeared
at the gym door.

'We are ready for the ceremony. If you do not feel ready, we can wait.'

I had been given a brief lecture on the background of Chin Wu and its
purpose, and an oath which I was asked to memorise. It seems appropriate
to repeat it here as it is an indication of the true meaning of the traditions
and the attitude demanded by its followers. It is very different from the
popular concept of flying foot and iron fist promoted for the theatre-going

Chin Wu crest: Crossed swords, the symbolic weaponry. 'To speak convincingly of peace, one must be strong. That is why every arm must be a spear, every hand an axe and every finger a dagger . . . that I may reach the top of the mountain.'

audience in the making of 'Kung Fu' movies. Brutality and violence are hardly conjured up by these centuries-old words devised in the monasteries of Shaolin:

'Hear me. Having been accepted as a novice of the Chin Wu school, I hereby give my word and pledge to abide by all its regulations and laws, to revere its ideals, to render honour and obedience to my teachers and to practise my art with all diligence, fortitude and patience.

I swear never to reveal the secrets of my learning to anyone without permission. I swear never to misuse the knowledge and the power that I will receive.

I swear to comport myself at all times with quietude and humility, that I may, through stillness, gain the peak of the mountain.

To witness this solemn oath, I invoke my lineage upon this earth, the generations of my ancestors. I call upon the forces that substance and move the universe.

So that if this oath I betray, their vengeance shall be upon me.

Help me!'

I was asked to write the oath on a sheet of red paper and to enter the gym with it when I had finished. The area was silent and black, lit only by the two red and gold dragon candles burning on either side of the shrine. From their light, I could see the four instructors sitting motionless and straight-backed on a bench against the wall.

The ceremony took perhaps ten minutes. I was led through it with whispered words and gestures from a senior instructor. Before the twin gods of Heaven and Earth, backed by the disciples of War and Peace, Violence and Non-Violence, I was asked to kowtow. With my forehead pressed to the floor, I repeated the oath and then, at a signal, burned it in the brass urn below the shrine. I then lit joss and presented it to each of the Gods in turn. The instructors rose with Master C. and presented me the honour of the Shaolin bow, the out-stretched right fist shielded by the curved, open palm of the left, symbolising the sun and the moon. Returning it as I had been shown, I was given the Chin Wu uniform and the card that registered me as a novice of The Chin Wu Athletic Association with its Hong Kong headquarters. I had arrived at the foot of the mountain.

In the many hundreds of times I climbed those still unswept stairs to look down from its windows upon the hustle of the docks, I learned a great deal that would be pointless and tedious to include in this book. My personal emotions along the journey back to good health are unimportant. It is enough to say I was a brother of Chin Wu and as such responsible for my own progress or lack of it. Patience, discipline and fortitude, the foundation that Mr Wu had so often mentioned, began to take on practical meaning. I will not pretend it was not difficult at first. The doubts, hopes, strivings, obstacles, misgivings and sheer lethargy that had to be overcome were exclusively my own.

The First Month

The first three training sessions at Chin Wu were given over to lectures on the origins of the school and the traditions of Oriental martial arts. A fascinating formula of Chinese characters, hexagrams, mystic symbols and historical dates would cover the blackboard, as the ancient sources of physical and spiritual power were carefully, if briefly, unfolded. The intangible was

The signs:
The sun/moon salute given by the Chin Wu Master and returned by his pupils.

The salute of reverence given by the pupil to the shrine on entering and leaving the class. Joss is also offered.

The nine-point star surrounding the sun/moon symbol.

explained, the mysterious revealed in transcriptions and translations of documents and scrolls as old as civilisation. Great Masters were talked of and their accomplishments discussed. Protocol was considered and observed.

We were taught to respect the opinion of our instructors as absolute; their attitude towards us, we were told, would always be tolerant but firm. 'You are all brothers. There is no competition among brothers, you will compete only with yourselves. There is no room for ridicule among brothers, only ridicule of yourselves. You must be gentle but stern with each other. Above all you must be gentle but stern with yourselves.'

No session began until each student had bowed three times and lit joss to the Gods of the Shrine on entering the gym. No session ended without the sacred salute being given by the Master and returned by his class. No student could leave the gym without bowing to the Shrine on his way out. We were taught the significance of the salute, the balled right fist shielded by the cupped left palm and held before you. This represented the sun/moon symbol of the ultimate Chi, the universe from which all power is drawn, and into which all power returns. The bow, so strictly enforced on entering and leaving, was the traditional Oriental prayer posture of palms pressed together and held before the heart with bowed head. This sign of absolute humility shared by Chinese, Thai, Hindu and many other Asian cultures, indicates 'respect for the light that shines within you' and is given after completion of any set of exercises. It is said also to represent the mountain which resides within each of us, waiting to be climbed.

Training began on the fourth session. Students were expected to attend twice a week and three times if possible. They were also expected to practise for at least an hour daily those exercises they had been taught and to demonstrate their progress at the next session. We began with the stances and postures, exercises designed to strengthen the legs and develop balance, position the body for movement and sharpen reflexes. They were extremely hard at first, being totally foreign to any stance or position one would normally take. We were constantly encouraged by the watchful and ever-patient instructors.

'It is good to stand a little discomfort. If there is no discomfort there can be no progress.'

'The heart of a lion cannot go far on the legs of a chicken.'

I sweated miserably and it seemed to me that I suffered alone. They were all so much younger, these rubber-boned Chinese and Filipinos. It was some time before I learned that they seldom sweat, whatever the effort, and that discomfort was not exclusively mine. Each novice endured in his own way. A wonderful feeling of comradeship quickly grew and was nurtured by the instructors. It was truly a brotherhood, one looked upon the other with interest and concern for his progress. Challenge was posed only by the will and the heart. Conflict only showed in each man's struggle with his own body and mind. It forged respect and liking that I had never experienced in any similar Western situation, and I had many a fo'c'sle, barrack room and bush camp to look back on.

The key to it all was patience. The Chinese characters for patience and fortitude were stitched in gold on crimson banners and hung throughout the gym, so that no matter which way you faced you could not help but see them. Of the class of twenty, three students dropped out in the second week, two in the third and another in the fourth. Master C. only smiled.

It is always the first month that is critical. Those that are still here after the fourth week will be with us on the twenty-fourth week.'

When the stances and postures had been thoroughly taught and practised at home or outdoors, they were tested for stability and we moved on to the sequence of warm-up exercises that are a prelude to every training session. With the stances 'beginning to take root', the warm-up exercises were not as difficult to achieve. Stiff joints, sinews and muscles, slack or taut through lack of proper use soon began to tone up with simple attention to neck and shoulders, arms, hands, waist and back, legs and feet. Each exercise was repeated sixteen times, counting under the breath one, two, three, four, five, six, seven, eight, eight, seven, six, five, four, three, two, one.

With the stances, postures and warm-up exercises well established by the fourth week of training, the class was considered ready to begin learning Pa Tuan Tsin — The Eight Precious Sets of Exercises. The history of these ancient breathing exercises was presented to us by Master C. with a sincere reverence which immediately set them apart from ordinary physical endeavour. The essence of Pa Tuan Tsin, he impessed upon us, was spiritual, and although its source was a gentle and a lucid one, its summit was the crystallised power of Chi. He rationalised this with an ancient Chinese credo which, roughly translated, went like this:

'In order to be gentle
one must be strong.
That is why each arm must be a spear.
In order to be strong
one must be prepared.
That is why each hand must be an axe.
In order to be prepared
one must be confident
That is why every finger must be a dagger.'

Many such axioms were used to demonstrate the health properties of these exercises and how they related to the violent aspects of the martial arts. They were, after all, no matter how humane their original purpose, the springboard for the most lethal and physically demanding procedure known to man.

The breathing exercises and the harmonious body movements that accompany them were taught slowly and methodically by Master C. They were checked continually by the instructors who measured the rise and fall of a diaphram with the back of their hand. The main problem, which seemed to be shared throughout the class, was shortness of breath. No-one seemed to have the lung capacity to accommodate the prolonged inhalation and exhalation essential to concentrated breathing.

'Never mind.' said Master C. encouragingly, 'After one month of practice each morning, your breath will be like the breeze through a pine wood and your step will be light as a child's.'

He was right.

I tell you this because, to a lesser degree, you will find the first few sessions similarly difficult. I say to a lesser degree because you will be your own taskmaster, less exacting and demanding of yourself than Master C. or the

Tolerance, patience,
determination.

instructors of Chin Wu would be. You will have no one to answer to but yourself, no instructor to face but the pages of this book, no guilt or disappointment in your efforts and progress but your own, no one to cheat but yourself. But that first critical month will be as much your testing period as if you are attending classes under their all-seeing eyes. It is from this self-control, self-appraisal and solitary judgement that discipline, willpower and certain success come with the practice of Pa Tuan Tsin. But first, there are certain basic things to be considered.

Facts and Fantasies

It is important to further explain why the images created by the Western concept of Kung Fu and those demanded by the words of the traditional oath are so tremendously different. There must be no confusion between the content and purpose of this book and the combat aspects of the widely publicised martial art shown on television, in movies and in scores of books and magazines.

Kung Fu (or the Cantonese pronunciation 'gung fu') simply means close application . . . to excel. It signifies dedication and skill, in a particular field. One can, to the Chinese mind, possess Kung Fu in cooking, sewing, sculpting or painting in exactly the same way as it is nowadays so spectacularly applied to the ancient art of Chinese Temple Boxing.

Kung Fu first became known to Americans in the early sixties, when a Chinese practitioner living in the United States published a series of books on the subject. His name was James Lee and his company 'Oriental Book Sales' was the first not only to print books in English on the art of Chinese Temple Boxing , but also to reveal the technique and detail of its secrets to the Western world.

He called it Gung Fu. About this time, the little known Bruce Lee arrived from Hong Kong. Already a master of several forms of martial arts, the amazing Bruce Lee soon became a popular figure among the Karate circles of America. Until that time Karate and the Japanese forms of Ju Jitsu and Judo were all that was generally known of Oriental fighting styles.

Incredible tales of Chinese hand-to-hand fighting had been filtering into the American Karate community from returned G.I.s who had witnessed it in the war theatres of Korea and Vietnam. It was said that against it even the lethal Tai Kwon Do of the Koreans was no match.

Bruce and James Lee decided to team up and, with James' publishing contacts plus the tenacity and talent of Bruce, they soon became the accepted authorites on all martial arts, which they called Kung Fu.

Violent epics, such as *Big Boss, Return of the Dragon, Fist of Fury, Shaolin Avengers* and many others, were soon demonstrating forbidden fighting techniques not only throughout the United States but upon every cinema screen in Southeast Asia.

Bruce Lee became the undisputed high priest of Kung Fu and the secrets of the Shaolin Temple, after eight centuries of carefully guarded silence, became available to the West for the price of a ticket.

Kung Fu 'clubs' sprang up throughout the Orient and from coast to coast across America. Very few of these followed the authentic traditions of the ancient Masters. Many short cuts were taken to learn forms: techniques such as White Crane, Tiger Crane and Praying Mantis, Go Cho, Wing Chun, Tai Chi Chuan and Pa Kau.

The result was that without the fabled patience and discipline demanded by the old Masters, Kung Fu, after its initial but quite long-lasting dazzle, had begun to fade as all fads do. Eventually, it fell into disrepute in the eyes of Western audiences as just another phase of Oriental violence and viciousness. The popular television series starring David Carradine at least made some attempt to associate Kung Fu with the all but holy order taught by monks for the improvement of the physical self and betterment of the human soul.

It is so very important, when contemplating the practice of Pa Tuan Tsin, that this violent aspect be totally removed, that it is necessary to look briefly at the origin of Kung Fu.

There has always been a great difference of opinion throughout the world of martial arts as to which of the many techniques came first. Which really was the original hand-fighting method that became known to the West as unarmed combat? Was it Karate, Judo, Ju Jitsu, Aikido, Kendo, Sumo, Indonesian Penjak, Thai boxing, French Savate, Korean Tai Kwon Do or Filipino methods such as Kuntao, Chako and Arnis?

The fact is that all of them sprang from the gentle art of Chinese Temple Boxing, or Wu Shu. For instance, Judo was brought to Japan by a Chinese named Chen Yuen Too during the Ming dynasty in 1558. He taught at the Asabu Shokokuji and has a monument at the Shokoku Temple near the Japanese Imperial Palace in Tokyo. Karate came to Japan from China through Okinawa and Korea and during the Ming dynasty many Japanese studied directly under Chinese Masters.

The best way to settle this long-standing dispute is to trace the course of Kung Fu's long history through the years to its original name, Wu Shu.

PART THREE

SECRETS OF SHAOLIN

*'Take the understanding of the East
and the knowledge of the West —
and then seek.'*
Gurdjieff

The Many Moons of Wu Shu

During the long and colourful history of China, many names and purposes have been ascribed to Chinese Temple Boxing and its numerous preliminary exercises. This history is worth tracing since it shows much of China's evolution since her first dynasty in 2200 BC. From legendary beginnings through feudal systems, wars and Cultural Revolution, the part that the original Temple Boxer played is worthy of note. Firstly, he was a mystic teacher of health preservation and spiritual arts, later an invincible warrior sought after by warlord and government alike. It was considered that one unarmed Boxer fully trained in the ways of Shaolin was worth twenty armed soldiers, and a recognised Master turned mercenary could ask his weight in gold from any general.

In earliest recorded Chinese history, this art was given recognition in the *She Ching* (Book of Poetry) as Chuan Yung, meaning 'Brave Fist'. During the Chung Chiu (Spring and Autumn era), it became known as Wu-I (Martial Arts). The period of Chan Kuo (Warring State) considered it Chi (Techniques of Fighting); the Han dynasty changed it first to Chi Chiao (Techniques of Ingenuity) and later to Shou Po (Hand Fighting).

The Han gave way to the Wei dynasty and it became Kung Shou (Empty Hand). It is thought that this name and period was the beginning of Karate, which was originally known as Kung Shou Tao. With the Ming dynasty came yet other names, firstly Chi Yung (Techniques of Bravery), then Chi-I (Art of Techniques). The advent of the Ching dynasty brought with it the name Pai Shou (Plain Hands). The Sung dynasty (960-1279 AD) has remained famous for its art, literature and philosophy. During this highly sophisticated period original health nourishing exercises were revived and developed as Hsing I (Internal Style of Wu Shu).

With the formation of the Chinese Republic and the gradual phasing out of ancient texts, character and cultural traditions, came Wu Shu (Martial Arts or Art of Combat), to become more widely known as Kuo Shu (National Art) and Kuo Chi (National Techniques). Of all these variations, Kuo Shu was generally accepted and used nationwide as a means of self-defence against foreign invasion. However, since the People's Republic of China's renewed overtures towards its Asian neighbours and the Western world, the Chinese have, for reasons best known to themselves, returned to Wu Shu, where it appears things may rest. Chairman Mao was largely responsible for its revival and today people throughout China, regardless of age, sex or circumstance practise Wu Shu as a part of daily life. As recently as 1977 Peking sent a delegation on a world-wide tour to illustrate the importance the Chinese place on good health through the cultural heritage of Wu Shu.

In further reference to the ancient art of Chinese Temple Boxing then, and so as to once and for all disassociate the pursuit of health and strength through Chi from the fighting form of Kung Fu, we too shall use the name Wu Shu for the remainder of this book.

To attempt to trace the true beginnings of Wu Shu one must remember that any such information which comes out of mainland China automatically comes up for question. The doctrine of Chairman Mao Tse-Tung wiped the slate clean of creed and custom, myth and legend, which had been so much a part of the Chinese spirit for centuries. Not much was left from the great book-burning to offer conclusive proof of any aspect of Chinese history. Records that did leave China were discredited and scholars were disowned. This was particularly so when it came to folklore or anything as shrouded and ancient as the source of the martial arts.

There is another reason, the Chinese say, for the lack of written evidence or literature on the subject of these arts. Since its earliest known beginnings, Wu Shu and its many diversifications were mainly developed and perpetuated by the illiterate or semi-literate classes, and therefore the information was largely disseminated by word of mouth.

A Master, or Sifu, was more likely to be found among peasant or coolie stock than among the wealthy or noble. The greatest Masters of all invariably emerged from the poor and hardy, the supposedly defenceless, particularly during the militant dynasties and the reigns of the marauding warlords of Imperial China.

The old Masters maintained that prehistoric man, forced through lack of weaponry to hunt, kill and exist in a predatory world with nothing but his bare hands and feet, was probably the very first martial artist. He was obliged to use his intelligence and strength as his only means of survival. Perhaps, it was then that Chuan Yung, the Brave Fist, was first raised in defence or deadly combat.

It is accepted by most military historians that no race on earth developed and perfected the art of hand-to-hand combat more effectively than the Chinese. In their 5000 years of invasions, civil wars and revolutions, the varied inventions of weaponry and fighting techniques were perfected and practised. Although these combat skills were no doubt introduced in the interests of self-defence, the warlord eras split province from province and separated soldier from civilian more completely than anywhere else in the world.

As far back as 400 BC, the Chinese peasant saw the growing need for unarmed defence against the well-equipped, well-trained soldiers who were never far away. Some say it is here that the first forms of hand fighting were introduced and recognised. They evolved into three separate systems with completely different goals: the art of health nourishment — the development of breath control combined with sinew stretching and muscular exercise for the improvement and prolonging of life; wrestling and hand-to-hand fighting — for the purpose of self-defence; and weapon fighting — the use of club, staff, knife, axe, sword, spear, lance, trident, bow and arrow for attack and aggression.

As to the origin of the exercises you are about to learn they are believed to have first come from India. The story goes like this: in 520 BC, a blue-eyed Indian Monk named Bodhidharma arrived at the Imperial Court of China to ask permission of Emperor Leung Wu Ti to teach Buddhism in China. It was granted and he made his way to Shung San (Mount Shung) and the Shaolin monastery. He is said to have meditated before its walls for nine years before teaching what he called 'The Eighteen Hands of Lo Han', 'The Marrow-Washing Course' and 'The Sinew Changing Course'. These were strictly health and inner energy methods taught to the celibate novice monks as part of their Buddhist training.

Romantic legend insists that Bodhidharma, known to the Chinese as 'Tamo' and to his disciples as 'Eyes of Eternal Summer', was also responsible for the introduction of the formidable Shaolin fighting forms. But documented scrolls prove that the first 'long hand fighting style' was attributed to a Master named Kowk Yee in the last Han dynasty (220-250 BC). So, it is unlikely that Tamo was the originator of Wu Shu or Pa Tuan Tsin.

After his death, at the age of seventy-six, the Shaolin monks Tamo had trained continued to practise and improve on his 'Health Nourishing Exercises', in the pursuit of peace brought about by perfect health achieved through the harmony of meditation and breath control. But, like so many things developed purely for good, it was not long before it was corrupted and turned against itself.

Growing harassment by bandits and renegade warlords caused the monks to channel their incredible powers into defensive combat techniques. By the end of the bloody Tang dynasty, their amazing skills and feats of courage and strength were talked about with awe throughout China. The tranquil monks of Shaolin had become the most feared warriors on any battlefield.

As their fame spread, word of their legendary encounters became associated with mysticism and the supernatural. Not surprising when you consider the superstition that surrounds all Chinese belief and the truly 'superhuman' exploits of the defenders of Shaolin. It did not take long for the rot to set in.

During the Ching uprising, after the fall of the Ming dynasty, patriots and guerilla bands shaved their heads and retreated to the sanctuary of the Shaolin monastery. There they secretly trained in the techniques of Wu Shu until the time was right to strike back at the savage Ching government.

A traitor among them betrayed the plot to the Ching administration, which sent its armies upon the loyalists in a surprise attack. In the battle that took place, the sacred Shaolin monastery was razed to the ground. For the few Masters who survived the attack, treachery and defeat served as a bitter lesson. They swore the secrets of Shaolin would never again fall into the wrong hands.

From that time, the strictest possible secrecy has been maintained. No student, no matter what his credentials, his social status or his fortune, would be accepted without absolute proof of his character and morality. This utmost caution was further protected by the severity of the oath* each novice was forced to take before being accepted into the Brotherhood. This close secrecy was enforced by the threat of death and damnation and was strengthened even more during the Boxer Rebellion.

*The oath on page 28, still in use in authentic Kung Fu circles, has probably changed a little with time, but its meaning is regarded just as seriously.

When the eight combined imperial armies invaded China and ousted the Ching government, foreign occupation proved little better or perhaps worse than the oppression it had replaced. Enslavement and abuse of the Chinese spawned a lasting hatred for the Foreign Devil, who had 'freed them from the claws of the Ching dragon only to be devoured by the Imperialist lion'.

That hostility led to a total rejection of any contact with foreigners and all things foreign; and recognition of or respect for foreign customs, traditions or religions was taboo. It is not surprising that China's most precious and enduring possession, the new, diverse and highly-effective variations of Wu Shu, was kept from foreign powers at all costs. The secret was, until recently, as jealously guarded as Western progress in the arms race and the conquest of space.

For the most part, this contempt and indifference still exists. It most definitely restricted traditional Chinese Masters from considering foreign students and does so to this day.

Only when super-hero Bruce Lee, the young, westernised wizard of martial arts, exposed all he knew in his screen spectaculars and began teaching American enthusiasts was the long-lasting taboo broken. Even so, at the very peak of his phenomenal and unchallenged success, he is said to have been asked to stop demonstrating his mastery to the outside world. No doubt he was reminded of his oath. The mystery that surrounds his death may have come as no surprise in certain traditional Wu Shu circles.

That, very briefly, is the story of Wu Shu as it is accepted by Chin Wu and other schools of equal repute. As with all attempts to define historical events in the China of old, this version stands to be contradicted. It is, however, an attempt to give as authentic an explanation as possible, based on the evidence and opinions of those who have devoted a lifetime to the preservation and continuation of a traditional art.

To return again to the exercises contained in this book. With the death of Bodhidharma and the several centuries of unrest that followed the corruption of Shaolin, a famous soldier hero of the Sung dynasty emerged. General Yeh Fei was, as well as a brilliant strategist, a great Master of Wu Shu and reputed founder of Hsing I (Internal Style of Wu Shu). It was he who revived Tamo's Health Nourishing Exercises and developed them. It was the great physician, Hua T'o, however, who devised Pa Tuan Chin which, loosely translated, means 'Pa' (eight), 'Tuan' (chapter), 'Chin' (different movements in a set). 'Chin' also means a very precious, multi-coloured quilted silk'. 'Pa Tuan Chin' therefore, means 'Eight Precious Sets of Exercises', or (roughly) 'Eight Precious Sets of Silk-Weaving Exercises'.

General Yeh Fei was a northerner and consequently Pa Tuan Chin became known as the Northern Style. It was considered extremely difficult to master. A less demanding Sifu from the south, known as Liao She Chiang, further refined the art of General Yeh, simplifying the movements with the same objective in mind: 'that of livening up the internal organs and arresting unhealthy symptoms in the human body'. Liao She Chiang's version became accepted as Pa Tuan Tsin, or Southern Style, and it is these exercises, unchanged for eight hundred years, that you are about to learn.

'Whoever practises Pa Tuan Tsin correctly will gain the pliability of a child, the health of a lumberjack and the peace of mind of a sage.'
Liao She Chiang.

Great Masters of Chi

Although this book deals with one set of warm-up and breathing exercises often adopted in certain authentic forms of Wu Shu, it in no way claims to be an introduction to the combat/defence aspects of the cultivation of Chi. If only for the sheer fascination of the subject, however, it would be a pity not to touch on the lives of one or two Masters and to give examples of the all but superhuman powers attributed to devotees of Chi.

Among the many schools and countless forms of Wu Shu practised throughout China and the Eastern world, many are becoming increasingly accessible to the West, and probably because of this diversification after years of secrecy, modified techniques and improvised styles are continually appearing. Some are created for expediency and to facilitate those impatient with their progress. Others are the legitimate advancement of new forms evolving from the ancient classics, often a combination of the best elements from several famous schools.

The best example of such a form devised by a modern Master is Jeet Kune Do, the deadly and spectacular technique developed by the late Bruce Lee. Jeet Kune Do means 'Fist Intercepting Way' and was used to shattering advantage in all of his films. It was arrived at through many sources, the classical and cultural as well as the experimental application of his own brand of genius. Only an artist of Lee's magnitude could have achieved such an ambition. In order to achieve it, he utilised a lifetime of practice, which included mastery of most known styles and methods including Karate and Tai Kwon Do.

He then made a long and careful study of the human anatomy, researched deeply into biomechanics, examined muscle function and nerve reaction in finest detail, so as to concentrate on the upsetting of an opponent's centre of gravity. His later studies were dedicated to the development of unique rotary movements as the most economical way of using energy to the greatest effect — as in his famous sequence of three continuous round-house kicks.

Lee developed a high-velocity 'internal punch' technique which left little external evidence but set up mass vibrations in the body that could result in internal haemorrhaging. Such unorthodox breakaways were heavily criticised by conventional schools for lack of philosophical basis and for their eclecticism. Despite this criticism, Jeet Kune Do became accepted as by far the most visually expressive style of all. It very soon eclipsed the highly contrived 'Chinese Sword Movies' that had for so long been the exclusive domain of Asian film-makers such as Run Run Shaw, himself a student of Wu Shu.

The persuasive and undoubtedly brilliant Bruce Lee soon convinced his director, Lo Wei, to do away with the picturesque weaponry and trick effects which had always been the most important part of the Eastern martial arts film and to bring things into the twentieth century by featuring the unarmed body alone. This would fully express the explosive force, control and grace that such action-packed epics called for. It is doubtful whether Bruce Lee or his director could have foreseen the personality cult that would arise from his decision.

Following the decline of Kung Fu movies came serious attempts to put things back in their proper context. The television series *Kung Fu*, starring David Carradine as Kwai Chang Caine, probably came closest to re-stating the age-old credo:

'Avoid rather than check.
Check rather than force.
Force rather than injure.
Injure rather than maim.
Maim rather than kill.'

This philosophy of patience was illustrated by Carradine's portrayal of an exile from the Shaolin Temple wandering through the American West, applying his temple training in a hostile environment with the humility and rigid principles of his Chinese teachers.

I once saw an excellent first-hand example of this same law of restraint which has left a lasting impression on me and set the seal upon my own code of ethics in such circumstances. It occured in a noodle shop in Manila's Chinatown where I was enjoying a bowl of conjee, or rice broth, with one of the Chin Wu instructors. His name does not matter as he was an exceptionally shy and humble man and would probably not like to see his name in print. I shall call him 'D'. He was a tall young Chinese of the classic Wu Shu build combining the grace and symmetry of a dancer with the defined muscle of a weight-lifter.

He was a champion of the formidable White Crane form as well as being thoroughly schooled in the Praying Mantis and Tiger Crane. This was due to his total dedication to no less that three hours solid practice every day, a discipline that had been religiously maintained from his boyhood. At the time, he was in his middle twenties and at the very peak of condition. The fine physique, incidentally, he claimed was owed largely to the constant practice of Pa Tuan Tsin, as he had never touched a weight in his life. He had recently returned from winning several honours at the International Martial Arts Competition in Taiwan. Master C. had told me this because, with characteristic modesty, D had not mentioned it.

The cafe was crowded with hefty looking Chinese truck drivers, sheet metal workers and factory labourers, and D and I were lucky to squeeze into a seat. We had hardly taken a mouthful when a giant of a man, wearing the grime of an iron worker from the nearby foundry, told my companion to give up his seat. I understood enough Cantonese to know that it was an order rather than a request and not a polite one at that . . . something along the lines of 'Why should a boy be seated while a man stands?' D ignored the insult, continuing to eat without acknowledging the remark.

The man laid it on a little thicker. 'Any Chinese who would be seen eating with a foreign devil is little better than a bar girl.' I looked around at the grinning horde and remembered that before the enforcement of martial law this area was noted for its rioting and violence. The man had a point. Seldom was a foreigner seen in the area, certainly not eating in a working man's cafe. To save the mayhem I knew D could cause in less than a second, I offered my seat. I was, after all, out of bounds. But the bully did not want my seat, he wanted D's, and was determined to take it. Reaching out he took D's bowl and emptied the contents into a spittoon with the comment that 'the boy would not be needing the rice because he no longer had a seat'.

It was a shameful insult, heard by the delighted crowd, which was on the intruder's side because of my presence, the man's size and D's youth. D could have redeemed himself in any one of a hundred spectacular ways, turning himself from a suspected coward into a hero with devasting ease. He did not. With polite apologies to me, his face a mask, he gave up his seat, purchased another bowl of conjee and ate it standing up. It was typical of the truly accomplished Wu Shu fighter, but I shuddered at what would have happened if the thug had laid a hand on my patient young friend. I encountered many such instances during my time with Chin Wu and it made me extremely proud to be even a very small part of such an elite group.

Of course, not all experts are as cool and considerate as the immovable D. The famous Johnny Chiuten, renowned as all-round champion of the Philippines in all forms of martial arts and technical adviser to Chin Wu, was also Manila's most notorious street fighter. This extract from a 1977 issue of *Martial Arts* magazine, written by an equally well known fighter, gives an idea of his prowess.

'The "old" Johnny Chiuten fought as if he were a bullet with blades. He came at you smiling, fast, hands and feet whirling until you were reduced to helpless, aching confusion; angry at yourself and awed by the man who had just mastered you. In those days I once had the honour of sparring with Johnny in the company of about thirty other martial artists. There were times when he would take on all of us, one after the other or four at a time, teaching us while administering formidable demonstrations of speed and power. We were not such a bad bunch of street fighters, counting among us several national champions.

Johnny Chiuten had his first lessons in Wu Shu from his grandfather in Canton. These consisted of breathing exercises and stances. Over the years his fighting style has become refined and polished to a unique perfection. All excess movement has been discarded, leaving a clean, irresistible thrust of amazing power. "My Chi", says Johnny Chiuten, "is a very young Chi."'

I had the unexpected honour to be chosen as Mr Chiuten's partner for a magazine demonstration of his art. I have seldom met such a polite and humble man . . . whilst, of course, he smilingly cut me to pieces.

In spite of remarkable experts like Johnny and D, the most incredible stories come from the past. Legendary Masters whose feats are still talked about in Wu Shu circles the world over. Accomplishments of Chi that will prove hard to believe for the average Western reader, in spite of what he may have seen performed on the screen by miracle men like Bruce Lee and his successors. Regardless of what perhaps he has seen with his own eyes at exhibitions of popular fighting techniques, he will find it hard indeed to imagine the extremes to which the ancient Wu Shu Masters so determinedly cultivated their Chi.

It becomes impossible to separate fact from fiction or myth from legend. Perhaps it is enough to know that the members of Chin Wu and other highly respected schools believe such stories absolutely and repeat them in lecture studies throughout fundamental training. For those who would like more recent examples, witnessed and recorded by one of the very few Western Wu Shu practitioners, with photographic support as proof, there is the excellent book, *Chinese Boxing: Masters and Methods,* (Kodansha, 1974) by

Robert W. Smith who, now in his later years, still teaches Wu Shu in his American school.

One of the best known and most fascinating stories deals with the origin and evolution of the classic Wang Lang or Praying Mantis form of Wu Shu, the style that has always utilised Pa Tuan Tsin as its life force.

During the Ming dynasty there was a native of Northern China named Wang Lang, a man of little means but great and genuine patriotism. From childhood he had hoped to be of service to his country but he was constantly rejected because of his tender age, mild appearance and slight frame.

Desperate to be of use in the growing unrest between the Ming government and the Ching rebels, he sought out the monks of the Shaolin temple and applied himself resolutely to the art of Temple Boxing. When the government faced almost certain defeat at the hands of the Ching hordes, Wang Lang, now a grown man and possessing the martial secrets of Shaolin, again offered himself as a soldier, but he was not accepted. He was rejected once more when the government was finally toppled and the infamous Ching reign began.

His determination to uphold his beliefs undaunted, he returned to the temple to further his studies and join forces with the guerilla bands plotting to destroy the new regime. Their plans were discovered because of a traitor in their midst and, as I related previously, the temple was burned to the ground.

Wang Lang managed to escape with his beloved sifu and they made their way across the Nga Mei and Kwan Lun mountains to Lo Shan in the Lo Province (now Shantung). He continued to learn from his sifu until the old man died, leaving a senior colleague to take over responsibility for Wang's tutelage. For many more years he learned and practised daily with his new Master, but was never able to defeat him. Finally, he was given an ultimatum. The Master would leave the student to his own devices for a period of three years and on his return he expected the younger man to defeat him with ease.

Left to continue his practice alone, Wang Lang was resting one day in the woods when his attention was attracted by a hissing sound. Above him on a low twig, a praying mantis and a large grasshopper were fighting to the death. He watched, fascinated as the powerful arms and chisel blows of the wary mantis confounded the grasshopper. How artfully it attacked and retreated at exactly the right time, grasped and released, feinted and struck methodically and relentlessly, until the grasshopper lay dead.

Wang Lang was greatly intrigued by the way the mantis had employed long-distance strikes coupled with sudden bursts of lethal in-fighting to deliver its fatal blows. They were the tactics, he realised, of a master boxer. Without further thought he captured the mantis and took it back to the temple.

Every day he provoked the insect with a piece of straw keenly noting the reactions and responses to such aggravation. Using his years of rigid training and practical experience, he soon discovered twelve principal methods of attack and defence employed so effectively by the mantis. He then combined these strategies with the finer points taken from seventeen other schools of Temple Boxing and consolidated them into one unique form, now known as the Northern Style Praying Mantis School of Chinese Temple Boxing.

Needless to say, when Wang's sifu returned and challenged his pupil to the decisive bout, the Master was easily defeated and immediately adopted his pupil's new style as superior to his own or any other he had encountered. They continued to polish and innovate, combining the strength and power of the mantis with the agility and speed of the monkey, until the older man died and Wang was left to pass on his knowledge alone. He chose the monks of Shaolin, whose order had given him so much in his early years. The art was practised in strict seclusion within the walls of the temple until Wang Lang died and an abbot named Sheng Hsiao Tao Jen began teaching the mantis style in other parts of China.

Among Tao Jen's pupils was an enterprising man of great strength who, having acquired the skills, established a 'pui kuk', or security service. Using the mantis tactics, he became known throughout Northern China as 'Li the Lightning Fist'. Many a robber band tried but none succeeded in subduing him and Li the Lightning Fist enjoyed a long life of fame and notoriety. Age forced him to pass on his skill to national Wu Shu champion Wang Yung Seng whom he had easily defeated and who had begged to be taught his amazing style.

From Wang it was passed on to the most colourful fighter of all; a huge northerner weighing well over 136 kg, known far and wide as 'Giant Fan of the Iron Palm'. Fan was a master of Tieh Sha Chang — a feat practised by thrusting the palms into a tank of iron granules — and possessed an 'awesomely powerful Chi'.

His strength was famous throughout China in the 1870s but was always only connected with self-defence or defence of the weak and helpless. Impressed by the passive character of Fan, Sifu Wang decided to pass on all he knew to this gentle and deserving giant. After some years of constant private instruction prior to Wang's death, Fan was crossing a field when he was attacked by two bulls charging simultaneously from opposite directions. Noting the angle and speed of each and with a coolness that is hard to imagine, he prepared to defend himself. The record claims that the first bull went down, pole-axed by a single throat kick, and the second from one blow on the spine. Both were dead before they hit the ground.

Such a champion was bound to become widely known in the way that legendary gun-fighters of the old West were known and pestered by glory-seekers. Fan was constantly accepting challenges and defeating opponents. Towards the turn of the century, he was invited to Siberia to take on the best Cossack fighters and Masters of the mystic martial arts of Mongolia. He beat all comers with ease. Then the Russians, with traditional style, trotted out their biggest gun, which they had, of course, kept till last. The pride of the Cossack cavalry was almost as big as Fan, far more ferocious and it was said that the combination of him and his great Siberian stallion was invincible against man or beast.

With a keen Russian sense of fair play, the horse and rider were pitted against the Chinese. Fan, it is claimed, stood his ground, summoned all his power with a perfectly timed breath and waited until his six-legged adversary was all but on top of him. Then, with a shout that echoed in the mountains a kilometre away, he killed the horse with a blow from his iron palm. The Russians capitulated and Giant Fan took the championship back to China.

It would be easy to dispute an example such as this on several grounds — even Muhammed Ali would think twice about making such a claim — and yet is is a reasonably modest one compared to many. As recently as the 1950s, jumps of six metres into the air and long jumps of ten metres from a standing position were being reported from Mainland China and Taiwan.

Even allowing for the exaggeration of enthusiasm and perhaps cutting such claims by half, they are still difficult to credit in the Western mind when compared to current Olympic records. Yet certain stories have persisted through the years and are accepted as gospel by the Wu Shu fraternity. Some of the most popular follow.

Yang Lu-Chu'an, the father of modern Tai Chi, who practised daily for most of his life and taught into his seventies, was said to have arrived at a friend's house after a three kilometre trudge through a rainstorm without a trace of mud on his boots. His son had demonstrated a similar buoyancy by rising to the ceiling to light a cigarette from the oil lamp three metres above him. Some fighters claimed to 'push' chairs and tables without touching them, even to walk up vertical walls.

The effect such stories of levitation and hidden energy have had upon the Asian imagination is dramatically demonstrated in Eastern 'sword' movies where Kung Fu warriors try to out-jump and out-fly the clans of the samurai.

Separating myth from fact is not so difficult when you are in regular contact with the Brotherhood. When I once watched with amazement as an instructor completed a series of push-ups on one forefinger, he told me of various methods once used to develop the power of the fingers for 'small hand' fighting in such deadly techniques as the Tiger Claw, Eagle Beak and Crane Beak. Possible for only the most advanced Masters, death is caused by striking the 'silent pulse points'. Called the 'Touch of Death' and fortunately, known only to an elite few, this power is easier to imagine when you have seen a man plunge his finger through a wooden plank or rip open a leather punching bag with a single jab.

One such master of 'touching' practised with a 20 kg weight tied to his finger and regularly set it alight with lamp oil. I have seen an old man squash a potato in his fist and then, to demonstrate his control, spar with an opponent while holding a bird's egg in the hollow of that same lethal palm.

Examples of Chi concentrated in the belly area are common at practice sessions. A man may invite another to strike his stomach or solar plexus and use the power of Chi to contract and expand iron-hard muscles to 'bounce off' his attacker, often with the result of a sprained or broken wrist or ankle. When you have seen a Wu Shu Master in his seventies run up the wall of a room, slap the ceiling three times and drop lightly as a cat at your side, it is all more easily believed. My own Master would occasionally demonstrate his Chi by 'pulling' a punch several centimetres from a thick plank of wood and snuffing out a candle on the opposite side with the force of its trajectory.

The examples are endless, each one seeming to outstrip the other. If those mentioned do no more than entertain and perhaps demonstrate the power attributed to Chi, when channelled into such force, they may also indicate its effect when developed for health alone.

Giant Fan, of whom we spoke earlier, continued to teach the Northern Style Praying Mantis throughout his lifetime and two of his students were destined to emerge above all others and to perpetuate the famous name of Chin Wu. Their names were Lo Kuang Yu and Lin Ching Shan. The dedication of these two fighters and the brilliance of their teacher reached the notice of the Shanghai Committee of the Chin Wu Athletic Association. In 1919, a contest was arranged between the two and the committee was amazed by the perfection of their style. The winner, by 'an almost mystic' margin, was Lo Kuang Yu. He was escorted back to Shanghai where he was made the Association's chief instructor.

In 1929, at the national championships held in Nanking, one of Lo's students, Ma Cheng Hsin, became the outright winner and both he and his sifu were hailed throughout China as the ultimate champions. Some years later, the Central Chin Wu Headquarters sent Lo on an inspection tour of its branches in the southern provinces, Hong Kong, Macau and throughout South-east Asia. He returned to Shanghai until war broke out and again was sent to Hong Kong to take over the Chin Wu branch there and to continue to teach the mantis style, which he did until 1944. From among these pupils there emerged a handful of men who are now the foremost Masters of the mantis form. Among them is Master Chou Chi Ming who in turn taught the art to Master Shakespeare Chan, from whom I was fortunate enough to learn, among other things, the precious exercises of Pa Tuan Tsin.

It is due to Mr Chan's confidence and generosity that I have been allowed to publish this book. 'Teach others what you have learned, but no more than you have learned,' he said when I asked permission, 'but teach them first how to breathe.' He then quoted a hexagram from *I Ching* (trans. James Legge, ed. Raymond van Over, Bantam, New York, 1969) which, roughly translated, meant

'I do not go and seek the inexperienced, but he comes and seeks me.

'When he shows sincerely that marks the first recourse to divination, I instruct him.'

Let us look then, at the first step along the road to Chi: correct breathing.

PART FOUR

THE GIFT OF
BREATH AND
HOW TO USE IT

'I eat the air promise-crammed.'
Hamlet.

The Meaning of Chi

This character represents Chi.

To the average person, respiration is the effortless, automatic process of breathing in and breathing out, neither helped, nor hindered by further knowledge or confusion. You breathe in fresh air and breathe out 'stale' air. It is what your biology teacher called oxygen inhalation (or inspiration) and carbon dioxide exhalation (or expiration).

Not many of us know or care much more than that. We take it for granted that this, along with other vital functions of the body, keeps us alive without our even being conscious of it. For the purpose of the exercises to come, however, it is enough to establish a few simple facts, with apologies to those who already know them.

There's a lot more to your lungs than two bags going up and down, day and night. For instance, the right one has three separate compartments, the left one two. The lower lobe, which you could say is the very bottom of the barrel, hardly gets used at all in normal, shallow breathing. It should be regularly reached, emptied of stagnant air and refilled afresh.

Each lung is infiltrated by the bronchus (bronchial tubes), leading from the trachea (windpipe) rather like branches spreading from the trunk of a delicate tree. From the branches, sprout the twigs (bronchioles) and at the end of the twigs grow the air sacs, made up of clusters of pouches (alveoli), rather like bunches of grapes. Oxygen is channelled via an intricate network of air canals from the larynx to the alveoli. If that oxygen supply route were to be cut off like sap on a vine, the grapes would wither and die. Add to this the scores of vital elements that make up and maintain the entire respiratory system and there's more to breathing than meets the nostrils.

We may not know it, but we breathe in two distinctly different ways for two totally different purposes, both at the same time. Air does not just enter and leave the lungs (known as external respiration), it also distributes oxygen throughout the body via the bloodstream, unlocking the doors of energy cells; this is known as internal respiration, or tissue breathing.

The simplest explanation I can give is this. We know our main source of energy comes from the sun. It is absorbed, trapped and banked for our benefit in all green plants by the process of photosynthesis. Much of the food we eat begins as green plant life: grains, cereals, fruit and vegetables. No matter how hard we may try to refine, process, boil and bother the life out of it, we end up with enough left to keep us going. This is excellent reason for increasing our intake of fresh greens, raw vegetables and fruit.

We also know that our bodies are made up of countless cells. What we may not know is that each cell stores a number of tiny 'powerhouses', called mitochondria, which have only become visible with the development of the world's most advanced electron microscopes. The rod-shaped mitochondria contain enzymes necessary to break down sugar and store it until it is needed. Oxygen is transported into the bloodstream via the capillary network. This is the internal respiration, which acts as a trigger mechanism, detonating minuscule explosions of sheer, exhilarating life force.

It is easy to see how and why our general health and physical well-being are directly linked to our capacity to breathe properly and to let the mitochondria do their work. This ability to control the process of breathing, to distribute oxygen to all parts of the body, to concentrate and release this power supply at will, is what the Chinese Masters call Chi.

It is a word that is often misunderstood, even among modern day Kung Fu practitioners; it remains a mystery to some. To most, it is simply a three letter word meaning physical power and is associated with health improvement and body conditioning . To them, the magic of Chi, with its legendary, almost occult, background, needs no further explanation or investigation.

The reason for this is simple. As with most of the martial arts, particularly the 'hard style', visually dynamic Karate, so-called Kung Fu clubs sprouted like mushrooms in the wake of Bruce Lee's fame. Often, these clubs were profit-making organisations offering crash courses in chosen techniques. They were not always under the supervision of fully-qualified instructors and seldom, in the case of Kung Fu, led by a recognised traditional Master.

A club that promises a black belt in a year or two, or mastery of a Kung Fu form in record time for a set package fee, obviously proves more attractive to the impatient student than the ten or more disciplined years of authentic instruction. In such circumstances, the time involved for fundamental training and conditioning is often skipped over, sometimes left out altogether or modified in the interests of getting on with the glamorous business of shattering tiles or performing flying kicks. Too often the main purpose is violence, whether 'defensive' or not.

The few schools lucky enough to be under the supervision of a recognised sifu attracted only those with the patience and genuine interest in the art as a culture rather than a street-fighting technique. These chosen few were fortunate enough to be taught the essential basics of Pa Tuan Tsin in the true pursuit of Chi. Even the little which has been intelligently written and preserved from Chinese history fails to define the true meaning of the word.

Chi is usually referred to as 'intrinsic energy', But what is intrinsic energy? Most dictionaries describe the word 'intrinsic' as 'belonging naturally, inherent, essential'; and the word 'energy' as 'force, vigour, individual powers in exercise, dynamic ability'. A reasonable interpretation, then, would be:
A NATURAL AND ESSENTIAL POWER OR FORCE INHERENT WITHIN THE INDIVIDUAL AND MOTIVATED BY DYNAMIC EXERCISE.

Probably the simplest and most accurate description of Chi is air pressure. Every movement or inner function of the human body, voluntary or involuntary, is brought about by manipulation of the muscles, which is impossible without internal air pressure. Bodily motion, no matter how insignificant, would cease without it. Active circulation of fresh blood, utterly essential to healthy tissue, is stimulated and regulated by this inner air pressure (tissue breathing) or degenerated and weakened by the lack of it.

Modern day exercises have their individual benefits and offer various advantages in the increasing drive to 'keep in trim', shed excess body weight or build it up, gain energy, reduce tension, improve digestion, purge constipation, lower blood pressure. The targets are endless and impossible to achieve through any one sport or single physical training method . . . except through the development of Chi.

Regulated breathing or breath-control is the basic aim of any athlete, whether swimmer, runner or weight-lifter. Any endeavour that calls for excessive bursts of energy or the storing and expending of reserve power under extreme physical effort has as its most important requirement controlled breathing.

The Mandala:
The Golden Flower.
Believed to be the most
resplendent of all flowers,
it is often used in Taoist
philosophy to represent
the flower of life through
breath.

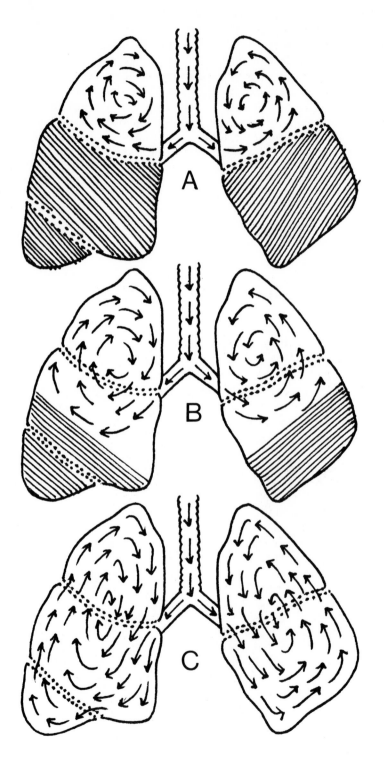

Breathing diagram:
A. Shallow breathing.
Only one third of the
lungs being used.
B. Middle breathing.
Two thirds of the lungs
being used.
C. Complete breathing.
Total lung capacity being
used.

The difference between concentrated breathing and other exercises is in the method rather than the aim. Top physical conditioning, robust health and long life are the dream of any intelligent human being. Chi makes this possible without the tedium of self-inflicted over-action.

The diagram on page 50 shows an unexaggerated example of the three breathing patterns: 1. shallow, or top, breathing; 2. middle breathing; 3. deep, or complete, breathing. The majority of people believe that they are breathing properly when they are inhaling and exhaling in the shallow manner illustrated in *Diagram 1*. Many of us are quite satisfied so long as we seem to be getting enough oxygen to keep us going. On finding that we puff and gasp for air when forced to run, climb stairs or involve ourselves in sudden physical effort, we say we are 'out of breath' or 'winded'. Our respiratory system struggles to take in the unaccustomed amount of air needed to perform the exercise.

In shallow breathing, only the top compartment (one-third) of the lung is used for fresh intake of air, the other two-thirds are left to stew in the stale air from your last exertion, and perhaps the smoke from countless cigarettes. It is significant to note that tobacco smoke is always inhaled through the mouth, the cigarette, pipe or cigar acting as the filter instead of the membranes of the nostrils. Most smokers inhale very deeply when they 'draw

Lung diagram:
Air travels from the nose through the windpipe, or trachea, into the bronchial tubes, which divide like the branches of a tree to form the bronchioles and alveoli, the tiny air sacs which distribute oxygen into the bloodstream via the capillary network. It is from here that the trapping and circulation of Chi begins.

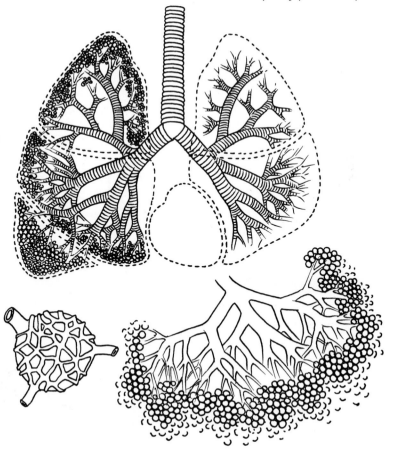

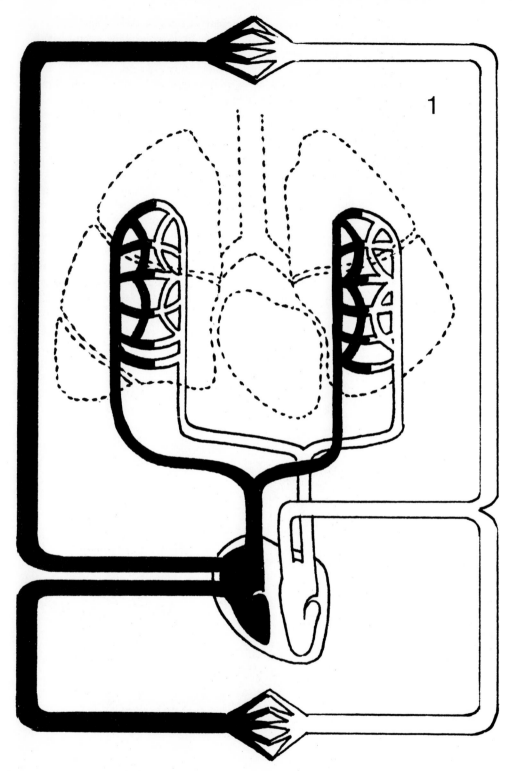

1

back' the smoke, but few expel it all before the next inhalation. It is not hard to imagine what effect this has on the intricate and delicate network of the lower lung; especially overnight, when a smoker usually mouth-breathes (snores) until morning. The part of the body upon which all else relies for energy has been left to stagnate, as the early morning cough and foul breath will testify. It is alarming to imagine what happens to these vital organs over a period of years and not at all surprising that smoking is connected with malignant lung disease.

Middle breathing, or perhaps we should call it 'ordinary' breathing, uses half to two-thirds of the lung capacity but still leaves the lower compartment untouched, especially the extra lobe of the left lung which hardly ever gets cleaned out and refilled at all (this area is often the beginning of trouble). At least middle breathing makes for a better balance of oxygen, supplies more energy and helps purify the blood. It is usually the physical worker, forced to take in enough air to cope with his task, or the normal exerciser, that unconsciously practises middle breathing.

Deep or complete breathing is obviously the way we were meant to breathe. If not, our lungs would only be the size of the unshaded areas in the diagram. But they are not. They are there to be completely and continually filled with fresh air and emptied. 'Not practical,' you may say. 'How can I sit at my desk doing deep breathing all day? My secretary would probably misunderstand me.' And, of course, you'd be right. We cannot consciously practise the complete breath throughout our daily routine, and deep breathing is a conscious effort, until it becomes second nature.

Lung/circulation: Diagrams 1 & 2: Impure blood (black) circulates through the intricate capillary system into the veins, which take it back to the right auricle and into the right ventricle. The pulmonary system takes over, pumping it through the arteries and veins to the lungs, where carbon dioxide is removed and replaced by fresh oxygen. Purified blood (white) then flows back into the left auricle and so through the left ventricle to continue circulation. Simple as it is, this diagram shows how vital complete breathing is to physical well-being.

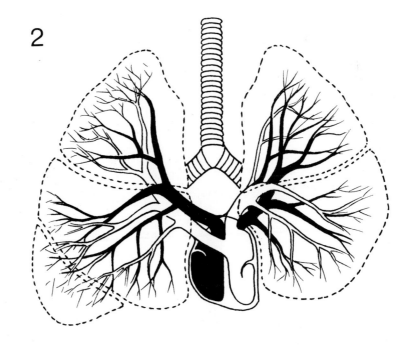

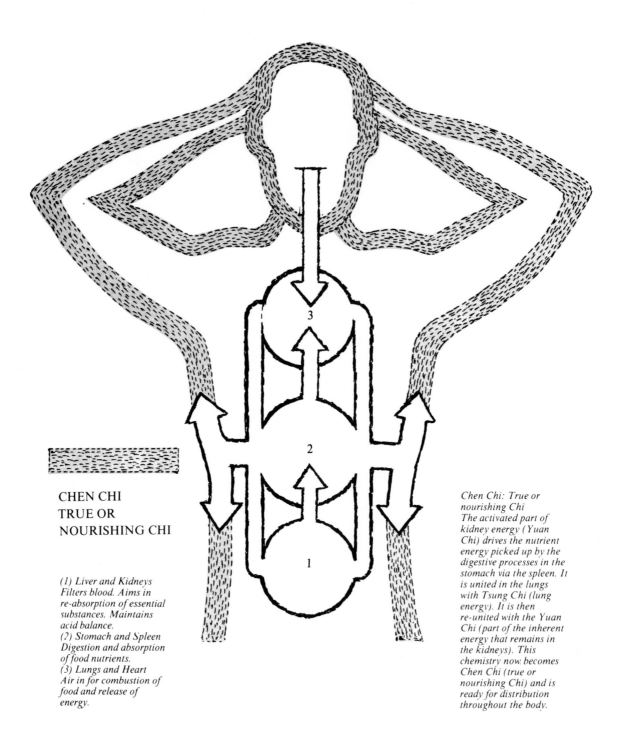

**CHEN CHI
TRUE OR
NOURISHING CHI**

(1) *Liver and Kidneys
Filters blood. Aims in
re-absorption of essential
substances. Maintains
acid balance.*
(2) *Stomach and Spleen
Digestion and absorption
of food nutrients.*
(3) *Lungs and Heart
Air in for combustion of
food and release of
energy.*

*Chen Chi: True or
nourishing Chi
The activated part of
kidney energy (Yuan
Chi) drives the nutrient
energy picked up by the
digestive processes in the
stomach via the spleen. It
is united in the lungs
with Tsung Chi (lung
energy). It is then
re-united with the Yuan
Chi (part of the inherent
energy that remains in
the kidneys). This
chemistry now becomes
Chen Chi (true or
nourishing Chi) and is
ready for distribution
throughout the body.*

No doubt in the days when man spent his time pounding across open country in pursuit of the sabre-toothed tiger, and then dragged it back to his cave after a fight to the death, heavy breathing was an automatic function. But if we cannot take off across the plains in search of action, we can at least go through the preparation before we begin our day. Even the greatest of all disciples of vital breath, the Indian yogi, realises this and begins each day with selected breathing rituals such as the 'cleansing breath'. This simply consists of raising the clasped hands above the head while inhaling deeply and then throwing the upper body violently forward and down to expel any stale air gathered overnight. Sometimes called the 'wood chopping' exercise because the movement suggests chopping a log, the cleansing breath is repeated a half dozen times at the start of yoga classes.

Only when we have learned to fill and empty our lungs in the way nature intended, can we begin to develop the inner, or tissue, breathing that leads to the cultivation of Chi.

The circulation of Chen Chi (the Sheng cycle) flows from the lungs, kidneys, liver, heart, spleen and back into the lungs. Some of it provides energy for the function of the organs and some is used in the external defence mechanism of the body (our disease resistance).

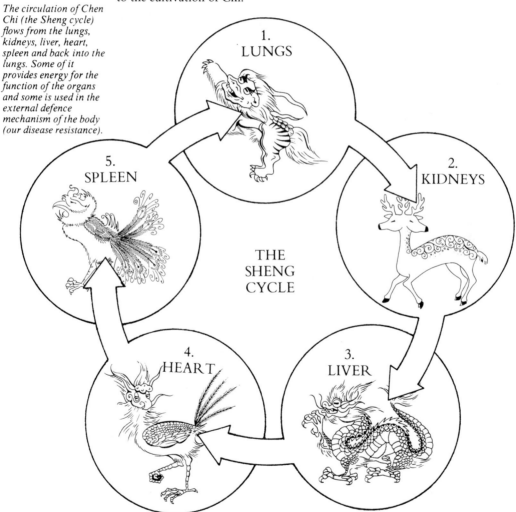

1.
LUNGS

2.
KIDNEYS

5.
SPLEEN

THE
SHENG
CYCLE

4.
HEART

3.
LIVER

Known originally as 'Chi Kung', the art of cultivating air pressure within the body, Chi is the practice of certain breathing techniques, beginning in the mind and eventually transported to the body's centre of specific gravity, the lower abdomen. This is a point 5–8 centimetres below the navel, which the Chinese call 'tan tien'. The person who accomplishes this technique preserves health, sustains youth and is able to call upon extraordinary reserves of inner strength. He can summon up split-second reflex action and explosive power, incomprehensible to the average human being.

Such a state is only reached by years of arduous and dedicated training and it would be foolish to pretend otherwise. There are many stages and variations in the climb to the ultimate Chi and there are no grades, distinctions or belts to encourage progress, only your own improving health and increasing confidence. Pa Tuan Tsin improves the entire body through relaxed movement combined with breath control, without sweat, unaccustomed pressure or the high degree of discomfort that normally accompanies intense physical exertion.

Perhaps now is as good a time as any to look briefly at what certain Eastern and Western experts say about the science of breathing. World-famous yogi, Selvarajan Yesudian, writes in his book, *Yoga and Health* (Mandala, London, 1976):

'OUR GREATEST MISTAKE: WE CANNOT BREATHE!
While we can survive for weeks without solid foods and several days without water, life without air is only possible for a few minutes. This shows that the connection between life and breath is the closest and that breathing is therefore the most important biological function of the organism. Every other activity of the body is closely connected with breathing. Breathing is of capital importance for our state of health, our emotional outlook and even for our longevity.
Civilised man does not know how to breathe! Our unnatural living conditions in modern city apartments and our cramped working conditions in factories and offices have resulted in our forgetting the rhythm of primitive breathing. Our stunted emotional life, and vacillation between passion and fear constrict our throats, and in the truest sense of the word, we do not dare to breathe deeply. The way in which children in this twentieth century breathe is scarcely enough for the merest vegetating. Their gasping is scarcely sufficient to keep them alive. How quickly this would change if people understood the ancient truth: only by the conscious regulation of our breathing can we achieve the resistance which assures us a long life free of sickness.'
The equally famous Hindu, yogi Ramacharaka, states in his book *Science of Breath* (Yoga Publishing Company, USA):
'BREATH IS LIFE
Breathing may be considered the most important of all of the functions of the body for, indeed, all the other functions depend upon it. Man may exist some time without eating; a shorter time without drinking; but without breathing his existence may be measured by a few minutes.
And not only is Man dependent upon breath for life, but he is largely dependent upon correct habits of breathing for continued vitality and freedom from disease. An intelligent control of our breathing power will lengthen our days upon the earth by giving us increased vitality and powers of resistance, and, on the other hand, unintelligent and careless breathing will tend to shorten our days, by decreasing our vitality and laying us open to disease.
The percentage of civilised men who breathe correctly is quite small, and the

result is shown in contracted chests and stooping shoulders, and the terrible increase in diseases of the respiratory organs, including that dread monster, consumption, "the white scourge". Eminent authorities have stated that one generation of correct breathers would regenerate the race, and disease would be so rare as to be looked upon as a curiosity. Whether looked at from the standpoint of the Oriental or Occidental, the connection between correct breathing and health is readily seen and explained.

The Occidental teachings show that the physical health depends very materially upon correct breathing. The Oriental teachers not only admit that their Occidental brothers are right, but say that in addition to the physical benefit derived from correct habits of breathing, Man's mental power, happiness, self-control, clear-sightedness, morals and even his spiritual growth may be increased by an understanding of the "Science of Breath".'

Such quotations could fill several volumes, being gathered from the writings of many great thinkers and philosophers of every nationality and from every part of the world throughout the ages. There is a similarity among them all when it comes to the question of breathing and its effect on our lives. Yet breathing has remained the least considered, the least important of all aspects of physical and psychological welfare in an age when we are desperately looking at every conceivable angle for improved living and future survival. We can only assume that because it is so easy to breathe 'normally', to just let one breath follow another, that the idea of controlling it for the benefit of our body rarely seems to be worth the effort. Unless, of course, we have a specific reason to develop diaphragm-breathing, as is necessary for singing.

The Chinese opera star for instance, is expected to keep up several hours of non-stop 'singing' commentary without appearing to draw a breath, the words and notes being linked endlessly together. To cultivate the lung power, they practise by facing a wall, a few centimetres away from it, and never allowing the vibrations or echo of their voice to die away.

To the Australian Aborigine the didjeridoo is a sacred tribal instrument. A hollow wooden tube up to two metres long (the sound it gives is very like its name didjeridooodidjeridooodidjeridooo), it must be played incessantly throughout a corroboree (ritualistic dance) to keep away evil spirits who will return once it stops. It has no reeds or valve holes and, unlike the bagpipe, no goatskin or bladder of air to store a reserve while the player draws breath. The honour of playing the didjeridoo is handed down by the elders to a chosen few who are trained as boys. They are given a hollow reed to blow through and told to sit by the edge of a billabong (waterhole) with one end of the reed in their mouths and the other well below the surface, the idea being that the air bubbles blown from the reed never cease. By constant practice the boy learns to inhale whilst he is exhaling.

To a lesser degree, the saxophonist, trumpeter or any wind instrument player must teach himself to harness and use breath to its fullest advantage. Perhaps that's why man who can summon up the breath to blow the alpine horn also makes an excellent yodeller. My own earliest breath discipline was as a fifteen year old ship's bugler. To develop 'breath-power', I was taught to practise with a sock stuffed up the bell of the instrument, although I suspect it had something to do with the noise I was making.

Although you may never have blasted or squeezed your breath through any kind of instrument, it is reasonable to hope that, as the reader of this book, you have given the matter of breathing for health more thought than is customary. No doubt then, you will have realised that there are certain things to be considered before we begin changing the rhythm of our breath.

Eating, Drinking, Smoking and Chi

Most serious exercise routines or forms of health improvement call for some kind of diet restriction or change in eating habits. This one does not necessarily do so. What, when and how much you eat is far less critical to a healthy system than an unhealthy one, and improved breathing is far more important than a careful diet. That is to say, a person practising Pa Tuan Tsin diligently is less likely to suffer the ill-effects of eating unwisely. Of course, the proper foods are of major importance to physical well-being, but a well-tuned state of health and a built-in resistance is better equipped to cope than a slack and sickly one.

Regular exercise of the right kind, taken at the right time and in the right amount, is the best antidote to illness. We know it is not as simple as it sounds. Life has spurred most of us from a walk to a trot, from a canter to a gallop, so that it's not that easy to slow down, stop, think and act. Unless of course, we are prepared to adjust our whole pattern of life: change our job to give us more time, pore over dietitians' charts, herbal tonics and the do's and don't's of health books that point out with frightening candour, the things we have been doing wrong for most of our lives.

Few of us are prepared to grasp the nettle to that extent. That is not to say that for those with the strength of purpose to discover and enjoy 'health foods' or even a vegetarian diet, careful eating is not of tremendous benefit. It is, but a healthy system comes first. Counting calories and cholesterol and balancing proteins may not be as vital to a long and energetic existence as some would have us think.

As a general rule, the strongest and fittest among us are those who work outdoors. But the number of such people is diminishing in the face of the rapid takeover of air-conditioned, computerised, mechanical labour-savers. Having worked in many outdoor jobs, I can promise you that a man who swings a 5 kilogram axe against a tree all day, swipes railway ties with a sledge hammer, drags a tonne or two of fish from the sea each night or spends his days chasing animals, can sit down at any time to some of the most unlikely concoctions imaginable, then sleep soundly as a babe and do it all over again when he awakes. You will often find such renegades battling on into lusty old age without so much as a bellyache, while their more cautious counterparts behind a desk develop ulcers, headaches, varicose veins and haemorrhoids.

I once worked with a lumberjack named Cauliflower Sid, who ate little but tinned cauliflower, as the ever-growing mountain of tins outside his tent testified. But he also felled more timber than men half his age. He was seventy-two and died at eighty-two after falling from a galloping horse. I have shared the dubious delicacies taken from fly-blown saddle bags with men who are sixty and as lusty as nineteen year olds. The fact is, the average lumberjack, cattlehand, seaman, soldier or labourer will often out-work, out-play and out-last his diet-conscious brother because his daily existence keeps him fit. With the greatest respect for health foods, such men have probably never heard of 'we are what we eat', otherwise they would all have gone to an untimely grave under a monument of empty cans, bacon grease, dried meat, hard tack and bangers 'n mash . . . not to mention strong tobacco and hard liquor.

Consider the huge work force of the Third World. Throughout the East you will find middle-aged to old Chinese women trotting up and down the planks of building sites all day balancing baskets of sand and cement; Indians, Indonesians, Filipinos and Malays labouring ten to sixteen hour days — all on a bowl of rice, a chunk of dried fish or meat and a spoonful of green vegetables if they're lucky. They smoke cheap cheroots, drink cheap booze, gamble half the night, bear many children and usually call it a day in their eighties, with a roomful of respectful great-grandchildren paying for a festive send-off.

All this should indicate that physical toil is nature's exercise which all of us were built to perform, and it helps greatly when it comes to avoiding the results of inadequate or unwise diet. How does this knowledge help us in our own situation, surrounded as most of us are, by a convenient variety of highly refined processed, frozen, dehydrated supermarket edibles?

If we are honest with ourselves, we probably accept that a dramatic change in our eating habits is unlikely to last. If there are certain things you really enjoy eating and that you have always eaten, giving them up altogether may not seem worth the sacrifice. Perhaps it isn't. With the tremendous research and millions of words written on the subject of 'eating for health', we all have a fair idea of what we should and shouldn't put into our stomachs. Many of us have been through the stage of the balanced health food diet; trundled off to the bulk store for our ration of brans, grains, dried fruit, nuts and nature foods. Who hasn't been frightened by the suggestion that we have been slowly but surely poisoning ourselves for most of our lifetime! But how many of us have stuck with a serious attempt to revise our daily menu. It's like smoking and drinking. It just isn't as simple as that! A sizzling plate of bacon and eggs with white toast and black coffee can be hard to reject for a bowl of wheat germ and raisins.

So we compromise and cut down, often only when we are advised to do so by a doctor. Sometimes, gradual change is far better than sudden denial. You don't confuse your insides or confound your palate by stopping a life-long custom.

If we are not prepared to take a course in mathematics in order to compute the exact measurements and balance accurate combinations, there is always a simple formula.

Eat less meat and more fish and fowl.

Eat less carbohydrate and more protein and grain.

East less processed food and more raw vegetables.

Eat less animal fats and more vegetable oil.

Eat less white sugar and sweets and more honey and raw sugar.

Eat less white flour and biscuits and more fresh fruit.

Eat less refined cereals and more roughage.

Now, to drinking. If we really want to know what alcohol does to our insides, there are many books on that disturbing subject. We don't need to be told that alcohol and serious exercise do not go together. One of the first warnings of Chin Wu is that of instant dismissal if the faintest whiff of alcohol is detected before a practice session. Refreshment during training is restricted to a large kettle of hot water or hot green tea (Ching Cha) from which students help themselves during training breaks (cold drinks are also forbidden).

What a person drinks in off-training time is his own affair, but he is strongly advised to stop taking liquor and never to drink anything ice-cold when hot. As with eating, it is the individual's choice and decision. Quite obviously, to quit entirely is best for the rehabilitation of the inner self. But again, let's be realistic. It doesn't matter why a person needs a drink or how many are needed to reach the desired effect. Be it relief from anxiety or depression, downright escapism, forced merriment, riotous behaviour or some good reason to celebrate, a drinking man is unlikely to stop for the promise of Pa Tuan Tsin or any other promise. At least not for long.

There is one very effective method of counteracting your intake and breaking down its harmful effects. It is not only a reconditioner of the liver and kidneys, where most harm is done by prolonged drinking, it is a health aid in itself and dates back as far as the origins of Wu Shu, although variations of it have long been practised all over the world with varying degrees of faith. It is the simple process of drinking a certain amount of pure water under certain conditions and at a certain time, known to the Chinese as water therapy.

Rather than attempt an explanation of my own, the following is a fairly faithful, if quaint, translation from an original Chinese document, in turn translated from a paper published by the Japanese Sickness Association in 1975. It turned up in Manila and copies were handed out to Chin Wu pupils with strong recommendations for its application during early morning practice of Pa Tuan Tsin. This is how the copy reads:

'This that follows is a Chinese translated copy of Water Therapy which was taken from a paper written by a Japanese author whose name is not known to me. I found the salutary and curative effects of this therapy not only by my personal experience, but also by those who know the treatment and were applying it without any let-up. I am inspired to translate this Chinese copy into English with the aim of giving it to those who have not come across this knowledge of God-given therapy, especially to the poor who cannot afford modern medication. This therapy cures at absolutely no expense except that of our faith and perserverance.'

The paper then went on to repeat a story which is reputed to have taken place long ago, and was apparently passed on by a very old but robust Chinese peasant. Some Chin Wu instructors, more from romantic imagination, I suspect, than from evidence, placed the events at 'more than a thousand years' ago. The full account is far too long and flowery to include here, but the following is a condensed version:

'For a long time I had been ill. I was unable to perform the smallest tasks. The fields and streams, the trees on the mountain, the plumage of the peacock had lost their colour. Day for me was night and night was day. Grasshoppers did not sing, nor linnets. No flower opened. Then, a man came to the door of my hut and asked for rice. He was old, he said, but his body was young and he journeyed for the love of journeying and lived for the love of living. I gave him rice and he cut all my wood in a very short time, also mending the shingles of my roof. Before he left he told me this: 'Tonight, eat nothing for your supper but fruit. In the morning as soon as you arise, go to the well and fill a bucket. Do not wash or eat but breathe deeply the early morning air and drink one gallon of pure water as you watch the sun come up. Do this every day of your life and you will never grow old. All sickness will be banished and you will find new life.' Then he went on his way, strongly along the path.

'Next morning I did as he had told me to. At first I found discomfort to drink so much. Many times I drained the cup. Many times I urinated and cleared my bowels. I felt a dizziness but still I drank. My conjee that morning tasted more delicious than ever before. After one week I could drink all the water easily. I urinated only twice, my motions were normal and my head was clear. I quickly became well again and I have never been ill since, not even with cold or fever. This happened thirty years ago when I was forty. Everyday, I have taken the water without exception and everyday is new to me and better than the one that went before. Now I live for the love of life and journey for the love of journeying. I tell this story to all who will listen.'

That is the gist of the document that created so much interest in the Chin Wu School in 1975. The writer goes on to say:

'Such claims for the drinking of water seem unbelievable and inconceivable, but facts prove it to be reliable and recommendable. Drinking sufficient quantities of water at one time renders the colon more effective in forming more fresh blood, known in medical terms as hematopoiesis.

This is made possible by the function of the mucosa folds found in the colon and intestine. These folds absorb the nutrients from food taken by our bodies and turn them into new blood.

Due to insufficient exercise of the colonic tract, man feels exhausted, becomes sick and finds his ailments hard to cure. Adult human beings have colons (or large intestines) eight feet long, capable of absorbing the nutrients taken by us several times a day. This nutrition is completely absorbed by the mucosa folds which in turn prevent or cure our ailments and are considered a principal power in the improvement of our health. Water therapy completely flushes this vital system in regular cycles, thoroughly cleansing the mucosa folds where dangerous waste otherwise gathers and remains.

In other words, applying water therapy will make us healthier and prolong our mortal lives.'

The paper then claims that water therapy as prescribed in the story 'deterred or benefited' the following complaints:

'INTERNAL AILMENTS

1. Headache, hypertension, anaemia, rheumatism, Bell's palsy, obesity, arthritis, tinitus, tachycardia, asthenia.
2. Cough, asthma, bronchitis, pulmonary tuberculosis.
3. Meningitis, hepatic diseases, aropathies.
4. Hyperacidity, dysentery, rectal prolapse, constipation, haemorrhoids, diabetes.

OPTHALMOLOGY

1. Opthalmic haemorrhage.
2. Opthalmia.

GYNAECOLOGY

1. Irregular menstruation.
2. Leucorrhoea.
3. Uterine cancer.
4. Cancer of the breast.

OTOLARYNGOLOGY
1. Rhinitis.
2. Laryngitis.'

The full claims of this unusual document are, of course, open to a great deal of speculation. Medical experts would most certainly question the variety of diseases it is said to repel. But the simple fact that no other liquid is known to be more widely beneficial or totally essential to mankind than plain water cannot be disputed. It is not only a reconditioner of the liver and kidneys, where most damage is done by over-indulgence, it is a health aid in itself. Plain, unadulterated water is as free and available to most people as oxygen. We have always known water to be good for us — which is probably why we stop drinking it as soon as we can when we are kids. We seem to associate it with washing our necks and invasion of that very private territory behind the ears.

Drinking large quantities of fresh, cool water by choice is fairly unexciting to some and its lack of popularity is not hard to understand when we consider the competition it has. The drinking tap is surrounded by so many persuasive alternatives. Even forgetting the addictive everyday drinks we are more or less forced to consume, there are multitudes of 'health drinks', flavoured and preserved milk combinations, canned fruit juices, bottled essences, powdered mixtures . . . so many things to mix with your water that the thought of drinking it on its own seems decidedly old- fashioned. Many of us go to our final resting place having never been closer to a regular water intake than cleaning our teeth and swallowing pills.

I have been practising water therapy for the past three years, until it has become as much a part of my daily exercise routine as the air I breathe. I can honestly report that, apart from the initial discomforts mentioned, I have enjoyed excellent health, despite my several daily pints of beer, dinner wines and nightcaps.

The procedure is simple. Boil 3.5 litres of water in a receptacle kept strictly for the purpose (so as to avoid impurities). Allow it to cool overnight and drink it during your first half hour of awakening. If you are lucky enough to have a schedule that will allow you to exercise on rising, then it should be drunk as explained on page 64. If not, get it down any way you can during your normal morning preparations.

For the first few mornings, you will probably find it too much to cope with. It may make you slightly dizzy or give you a touch of headache. It will certainly loosen your bowels in a hurry, probably several times. Don't worry, it should if it's working. You will also urinate frequently and fully for an hour or two.

If you cannot consume the full quantity, drink as much as you feel you can and increase on following days. Do not worry if you vomit at first, it is only pure water. You should try to reach at least 1.5 litres with ease within the first week and 2.5 litres by the second. You may wish to ask your doctor what he considers your particular intake should be and his opinion of the treatment in your case.

If you decide to try water therapy, it is vitally important that you do not miss a morning and therefore break the cycle. After three or four weeks, you will find it as much a part of your ablutions as visiting the bathroom.

Do *not* put the water in the fridge. Drink it warm rather than very cold. If you believe in nothing else, you will find that you can take your usual intake of alcohol with less effect, hangovers will be a thing of the past and you will know that your liver and kidneys are being thoroughly taken care of. Water therapy is not an essential part of Pa Tuan Tsin but the drinking of some water, however little it may be, is strongly recommended during the exercise period.

Smoking cigarettes, cigars, pipe tobacco or anything else you habitually draw into your lungs, cannot possibly help in the development of any form of respiratory exercise and health improvement: the cutting down or cutting out most certainly will.

As with alcohol and junk foods, it is a question of degree. It is also an undeniable fact that some people happily smoke their lives away to a ripe old age while others choke it away long before they should. There will always be the popular argument among heavy smokers that they could give up smoking, walk outside and get run over by a bus or that a lungful of polluted city air, diesel fumes, chemical waste, factory smoke, jet vapour, not to mention nuclear fallout and regular doses of carbon monoxide, could do them more harm than a six month supply of tobacco. Printed health warnings and the ban on television advertising don't do much to convince a confirmed smoker. Even hideous films of a heavy smoker's lungs shown on a screen will at best make them sweat a little—and fumble for a nerve stick when the lights go up.

In these days of high stress points and low resistance, increased anxiety factors and mounting psychological strain, it is not surprising to find the number of people lighting up greater than the number giving up. So, as with the excesses of tasty food and good liquor, it is pointless suggesting that you cut it down or cut it out. You know by now what your two packs a day are doing to you and you don't need anyone to remind you—the hacking and barking you do each morning over the wash basin does that, so does the taste in your mouth and the shortness of your breath.

What may make you think twice is the difficulty you will find when trying to prolong your breath intake. A non-smoker can quite quickly develop inhalation and exhalation of thirty seconds plus. If you are a heavy smoker, ten seconds may well be your limit. Almost certainly, if you take Pa Tuan Tsin seriously, you will automatically begin to cut down. First, you will avoid your early morning drag in preparation for exercise: the exercises themselves prohibit smoking during practice. You are unlikely to feel like one directly afterwards and may be well on your way to the office or half-way through the morning before you find yourself reaching for the cigarettes.

When Pa Tuan Tsin has become a regular part of your routine, say in the second or third month, the effects of increased oxygen and controlled breathing will prove so much more beneficial to peace of mind and bodily well- being that you may finally give up altogether.

The Time and Place

Now that we know a little about the exercises and the do's and don't's that go with them so far as eating, drinking and smoking are concerned, there are one or two other simple but very important questions to consider. First, what is the best time to practise Pa Tuan Tsin?

The ideal time for breathing exercises, the Masters say, is between 1 a.m. and 3 a.m. This might have been fine for the Shaolin monks, but they didn't have colour television and probably went to bed at sundown. Also, most of their true rest came from advanced meditation. They had reached a state of Chi that called for no more than three to five hours' sleep.

To bring things up to date: unless you are having difficulty with sleep (in which case, fifteen minutes or so of breathing exercises can do wonders), early morning is by far the best time (as early as your daily demands allow), or second best, late evening.

First, for morning breathers. We all differ in our waking habits, some are fresh and energetic while others take an hour to get moving. Whichever you are, as your enthusiasm grows with progress, you will find it becomes easier to rise early, feeling refreshed and eager to exercise at 5 a.m. When the world is still asleep, nothing could be better. If not, as close to it as you can manage without destroying your whole routine.

The benefits of the early morning are obvious. The air, whether you are in Pittsburg or Putney, is at its best and distraction is at its lowest. So, for early morning breathers the ideal time is on rising, as early as possible, and finishing in time to allow half an hour before eating and fifteen minutes before bathing. *Do not shower or bath for at least fifteen minutes after finishing your exercise. When you do, make it a warm or hot one, never ice-cold. Allow at least half an hour before breakfast. Never nibble or sip during exercise unless it's cool to warm water or clear Chinese green tea.* (You can buy 'Ching Cha' from any Chinese store and many supermarkets).

If circumstances make it easier for you to be an evening breather, your best time is an hour or so after dinner or within a half hour before going to bed.

THE IDEAL ROUTINE. On rising, drink two or three glasses of water, visit toilet. Do not wash thoroughly, just sluice the face and solar plexus with cold water. Warm-up exercises for fifteen minutes. Brief rest. *Do not sit down.* Breathing exercises for fifteen minutes. Brief rest: ten minute walk (or just move around). *Do not sit down.* Prepare for shower or bath. Eat breakfast.

The length of time you spend on Pa Tuan Tsin will increase with your progress. As a beginner, you should allow twenty to thirty minutes slotted into your day.

The best place to practise Pa Tuan Tsin depends on location and surroundings. The essentials are freedom from interruption and any form of distraction. If you have a garden, select a spot in it. If you know of a place within easy reach, a park, a field, a beach, aim for it. If you live in a high-rise building, the open window of your bedroom with the door locked will do nicely.

It is easy to imagine how simple it was for the monks of Shaolin in the scented gardens of their mountain retreat, watching the sun rise like a gong. Nothing bigger than the birds and bugs to contend with. What about early traffic? Kids? The neighbour's radio? All you can do is find the quietest and most private place your particular world allows . . . the best available air and the least chance of distraction. *Use the same spot every day, facing the same direction.* Fix your attention on some object and don't lose it . . . a flower, a leaf, a distant cloud, anything that is quiet and natural.

THE IDEAL SITUATION
Quiet and private as possible.
Best available air.
Same spot and direction.
Concentrate on one pleasant object.
Rid the mind of all else.

If you follow this routine without breaking it for the first month, you will find the mind and body beginning to work as one, the exercises will seem to take control and your mind will go along for the ride. It is a wonderful feeling of true relaxation and growing strength. Two additional rules which only you can insist upon are consistency and mental attitude. Consistent practice and positive thinking.

For the quickest and most definite results Pa Tuan Tsin should be practised every day, and this is what you should aim for. If you feel at first that this is too much, begin with every other day, or even two to three times a week will do. Your own progress will increase your stamina, your enthusiasm and your frequency. Once a day-to-day pattern is achieved, try not to break it. It is inadvisable to perform Pa Tuan Tsin in any state of anxiety, distress or excitement. It is better not to try. You will know if the disturbance is stronger than your will in the first five minutes. Don't persevere. If you find your thoughts competing unsuccessfully with your exercise, *stop. Don't fight or work at it.* The essence of Pa Tuan Tsin is quietude and relaxation.

WHAT TO WEAR. Whatever is loose-fitting and comfortable is the correct clothing for the practice of Pa Tuan Tsin. A track suit is fine if it is cold, pyjamas are ideal if you are indoors. An old pair of pyjama trousers and a tee-shirt will suffice if the weather is mild and you practise outside. It is not advisable to practise stripped to the waist until you are well advanced. Initially you may sweat, which can leave you liable to chill.

Never exercise with a leather or stiff belt, this not only interferes with breathing but can be dangerous to internal organs, especially when practising deep bends. A sash, old scarf, necktie or any sort of soft cord is comfortable without restricting freedom of movement. Footwear should be soft and preferably without heels, rubber soles or any non-slip soles. Avoid plastic. The traditional black, elastic-sided Chinese slippers are best, easily found in Chinese stores. Tennis or track shoes or perhaps an old pair of carpet slippers is a good alternative. Remove your wristwatch, neck chain, rings or any other accessories you may be in the habit of wearing. If your hair is long, the wearing of a sweat band around the forehead is a good idea.

You are ready to start your first Pa Tuan Tsin practice session. You may or may not have found it necessary to practise the simple deep breathing exercises mentioned on page 55 in order to increase your lung capacity.

The demonstrations in the illustrated section which follows have been separated into four parts: 1. Stances; 2. The Warm-up; 3. Pa Tuan Tsin; 4. Extra Exercises.

Remember: Patience
Discipline
Fortitude
Confidence.

PART FIVE

THE PREPARATION

'Silently thou fliest upward in the morning.'
The Book of the Seal of the Heart.

The Stances

Correct stances are an essential part of all Wu Shu training and vital to Pa Tuan Tsin if it is to be practised correctly and to its full advantage. The way we stand, the exact position of our feet, the posture of trunk, shoulders and head should be practised and perfected first. Their purpose is to strengthen the legs and lower trunk, improve balance and agility. In combat Wu Shu, this concentration of Chi in the lower body is channelled into amazing leaping and kicking power. Our purpose is a far gentler and more beneficial one, so let's get started on the fundamentals.

All foot and leg positions play a most important part in the exercises. Think of them as the basic steps in military drill as taught to a rookie in Boot Camp . . . standing to attention, properly at ease, right, left, about-turn and so on. Remember also that agility begins and ends with the legs. If the leg muscles are strong, sinews supple, ankles, knees and hip joints mobile, your every step becomes lighter; to walk run or jump becomes a pleasure rather than an effort.

You may already possess a pair of sturdy legs with good thigh and calf muscles developed and maintained by regular rounds of golf, chasing a tennis ball, swimming, jogging or any other method of building leg power. If you have, you will no doubt find these stances easier to master than someone who has not. The stances may look simple and elementary to an athlete, but it is best not to underestimate their effectiveness until you have tried them and learned to hold them steadily for the required periods of time.

Each stance is based on concentrating the strength of one leg against the other, by the shifting of bodyweight with precise footwork. When practised properly, a minute or two in a particular stance can have the same result as a half-dozen turns around the block or running up and down a flight of stairs.

Correct posture is also essential. You may find it a little awkward at first, remembering to keep head, back, elbows, shoulders and stomach at the correct angles, at the same time concentrating on the positioning of your feet and legs. Your body will very soon respond and straighten to its natural points of balance much in the same way as it does when riding, dancing or swimming. The stances are all natural movements and your body will adjust and co-ordinate accordingly.

As there is no instructor to square a shoulder, tuck in an elbow, straighten a neck or back, pull a stomach into line, bend a knee or position a foot, you must check your own stance. Until you become naturally and comfortably accustomed to it, it is very helpful to practise in front of a full-length mirror.

Progress in the stances, once you have them right, is measured by the time for which you can hold them. In the early stages, you may find it difficult to hold a stance for more than a few seconds. This does not matter. Keep a stop-watch or clock with a second indicator where you can see it. A few seconds gained each day or even each week is all you need. If you have had any previous leg, back or internal injury (such as hernia) it may be wise to show the stances to your doctor and seek his approval before throwing yourself into them. After a month of practice, you will find that which was unendurable after thirty seconds is now comfortable for up to several minutes. You may find it necessary to practise the stances for the first week before beginning Pa Tuan Tsin.

Here they are, then, beginning with the foundation stance upon which all others are built and from which they are all reached, the Horse Stance.

The Horse Stance

The Horse Stance is the rock upon which most Wu Shu forms are built. It is the stance mentioned on page 70, which the old Masters had their pupils practise for up to three years before deciding if they were worth teaching further. When the Horse Stance is perfected, nothing and no-one can shift it . . . which is perhaps why it is also the basic fighting stance.

It is called the Horse Stance simply because the posture is that of riding an invisible horse. The feet are wide apart, the knees bent and the seat lowered into a non-existent saddle, whilst the hands grip imaginary reins in what is known as the Punch Posture.

Apart from its importance to balance, the Horse Stance begins to give immediate benefit to general health. It strengthens the legs evenly, developing reflex stability and making it less likely for you to trip, fall, be pushed or knocked down. It greatly improves circulation, aids digestion and ends constipation.

The very first step is to find the exact point of balance for your particular weight and size—which means deciding the correct distance that your feet should be apart. This is done by measuring or 'opening' the stance with your feet, as shown in the diagram. Once this is discovered, the need to measure your distance can be dispensed with as practice continues. By the end of the second or third week, you will be able to open your stances comfortably and naturally, as you become familiar with your invisible horse.

With the feet properly spaced and toes pointed straight to the front you allow the knees to bend and lower yourself into the sitting position. At first, you may find a tendency to lean forward but gradually (some faster than others), you will learn to straighten in the 'saddle' and sit back comfortably. With the stomach in, the back, head and entire upper body will be in a straight line when viewed from the side. It may take a while to achieve this erect posture and perfect it but, remember, each time you practise it the effort is doing you good.

1

3   3

2   1   1   2

2   3

You will also find that, no matter how athletic you are, the Horse Stance will tire you fairly quickly: your thigh muscles will ache and you will feel the urge to straighten up to relieve it. It is the willpower to ignore this urge, to persevere a little longer (always within your own limits) that develops the stance.

The ultimate question in the Horse Stance is how low you can go. The lower the stance the better its effect, but this takes time. Don't worry if at first you feel 'tall in the saddle' and don't force yourself to a point of over-exertion. It is better to practise in a higher (Half-horse) position, and gradually lower a little at each session, than to subject yourself to too much strain too quickly. As your legs strengthen, you will find yourself lowering the stance easily and automatically.

Another and slightly more urgent question you will find yourself asking is 'How long am I expected to hold this position?' Again, this is a matter of individual effort. The answer is 'As long as you can, with as much initial discomfort as you can stand without overdoing it.' There is no yardstick but your own. It is just as well to remember that no progress is possible in any form of exercise without continued effort. Perhaps it's worth mentioning that an advanced Wu Shu practitioner can hold the Horse Stance indefinitely and would think nothing of a half an hour without shifting.

If you can build up to, say, five minutes in the first few months, you will be doing very well. A clock with a second-hand will tell you how you are progressing. So long as you add a few seconds each day or even each week, you are making progress. *It is better to begin with a higher but correct stance for longer periods than a lower, incorrect stance for short exhausting bouts.*

When the stance is perfected, it forces Chi down to the lower abdomen and is distributed between the spread legs to the feet. It makes for perfect stability, ease of balance and a lightness of movement you will never have experienced in normal motion.

The Bow Stance

The Bow Stance is so called because the widespread feet and stretched legs, one straight as an arrow, the other bent and the body curved, could be seen as a fully drawn bow, its shaft poised for flight. This is not an exaggerated interpretation. The Bow Stance, when applied to the fighting technique, is used to launch an attack, the rear leg firing the strike deep into an opponent's defences.

Its purpose for us is far less aggressive. The Bow Stance is designed to further promote solid balance and strengthen both legs. As a variation of the Horse Stance it eventually leads to the 'rooting' of Chi, making it almost impossible to lose balance.

Until you become accustomed to opening the Bow Stance accurately and comfortably it is best reached through the Horse Stance:

1. Open your Horse Stance.

2. Pivot to the left on the soles of the feet until the right leg is straight at the knee, toe pointing to 11 o'clock. The left leg is bent as far forward as possible, toe pointing to 9 o'clock. The trunk is upright from the waist, arms and shoulders drawn back hard (but relaxed). Eighty per cent of the body weight is thrown forward on to the bent left leg. Hold the stance for as long as possible. When the weight on the left leg becomes excessive, pivot back to the Horse Stance *without raising the head level or rising on the knees.*

3. Take a long deep breath. Exhale steadily.

4. Repeat the same pivoting movement to the right. Remember not to ease the stance by raising the head and knee level.

At first, you may find moving from Horse to Right Bow, to Horse, to Left Bow without rising too difficult. If so, don't worry, settle into each stance in the way most comfortable to you until you are able to complete all three movements without rising. Hold the stance for a minute or two, extending your time as best you can.

The Seven Star Stance

The Seven Star Stance is considered the classic fighting stance of the Northern Shaolin school of the Praying Mantis. It is an attack stance from which the 'short hand' close range engagement is launched, the right heel often used as a strike against an opponent's instep or a scoop to unbalance him. Our less formidable purpose is to further perfect balance and strengthen leg work.   The Seven Star is also opened from the Horse Stance.

1. Keep shoulder, elbows and fists tucked into the punch posture. Leave the left foot where it is without shifting its position.

2. Lean eighty per cent of the bodyweight on to that left leg, bending it accordingly. Stretch the right leg, rigid and locked at the knee, resting lightly on the heel of the foot. Upper body twists to face the right in line with the up-raised toe. When the stance is correct, most of the body weight will be taken up on the half bent left leg. The right heel will be lightly resting on the floor.

3. Hold the stance for as long as is possible. Shift back to the Horse Stance.

4. Inhale deeply. Exhale steadily. Reverse into the left Seven Star position.

You must expect to find this stance quite difficult to maintain for any length of time because of strain on the bent leg. Be patient and gradually increase the seconds as the legs become stronger.

The Half-knee Stance

The Half-knee Stance is a variation of the Seven Star. It is simply a feinting manoeuvre intended to give the opponent the impression of retreat while remaining poised to spring from the bent back leg.

1. The Seven Star Stance is adopted.

2. The right leg is drawn back until the knee is half bent and the toe rests very lightly on the floor. Again, most of the body weight is taken by the 'springing' leg.

3. Hold the right Half-knee Stance for as long as possible and reverse to the left.

The same degree of strain will again be placed on the prop, or spring, leg. The outstretched toe should be so lightly poised so as to pass a sheet of paper beneath it. At first this toe (pointed in much the same way as a ballet dancer) may rely on too much pressure against the floor; this will ease as the spring leg learns to take more and more weight and balance upon itself. Think of it as a tight-rope walker feeling for his next step.

1

2

3

4

The Front Cross Stance

The Front Cross Stance is an evasive tactic which develops great agility. It is essentially another leg and balance exercise which, although not utilised in Pa Tuan Tsin, is a very worthwhile part of your programme. Aimed at an opponent attacking from the side, it advances swiftly under the attacking guard and offers a low strike.

1. From the Horse Stance. Keep shoulder, elbows and fists in the punch position.

2. Bring the left leg across the right knee and sink into a crouch. Left foot flat on the floor, toe at 9 o'clock, right heel raised, toe at 11 o'clock. Body weight is evenly distributed on both legs. Hold as long as possible.

3. Regain Horse Stance.

4. Reverse to left Front Cross.

1

2

3

4

The Back Cross Stance

The Back Cross Stance is a similar evasive tactic, this time defending to the front with the same effect.

1. From the Horse Stance and punch position.

2. Cross the left leg behind the right, left heel raised, toe at 12 o'clock. Right heel flat, toe at 11 o'clock. Sink into a crouch position. Upper body facing front.

3. Regain Horse Stance. Inhale deeply. Exhale steadily.

4. Reverse to right Back Cross.

Both of these exercises are particularly hard on the legs at first and you may find it difficult to retain balance. After a few weeks of practice, however, you will be able to slip from one to the other without rising.

Once the stances are understood and you find you can open them quite easily, you can progress to the warm-up exercises.

1

2

3

4

The Warm-up Exercises

The warm-up exercises are really the limbering-up process before the practice of Wu Shu proper. They are a prelude to the Chien Taos, which are dance-like movements performed in continual sequence. They will become second nature before being applied to actual sparring sessions. It is much as a ballet dancer will go through a stretching routine on the bar before a performance, or a boxer will warm up on the speed ball before a fight. As such, the warm-up is not essential. You can perform Pa Tuan Tsin without it. It is, however, a highly effective way of getting your circulation going, taking out any kinks in your body and preparing your mind for concentration.

The warm-up is a sinew-stretching and muscle-loosening procedure designed to minimise strain, starting with the head and neck, arms and shoulders, waist and abdomen, legs and feet. The full set of eight warm-up exercises each repeated eight times will take no more than fifteen extra minutes and is well worth making time for if you can.

In the beginning, the warm-up exercises should be approached carefully and without impatience. Remember, you are testing yourself joint by joint, sinew by sinew, muscle by muscle. Even if you are fit and accustomed to regular exercise, there may well be effort involved with which your body is not familiar. A pulled muscle or sprained sinew is not only a very painful way of interrupting your progress but, without the advice and encouragement of an instructor, it can easily dampen your enthusiasm to continue.

Bear in mind that, no matter how receptive or flexible your attitude may be, however firm your resolution, there will be times in the first few weeks when you will be sorely tempted to drop out. The only way to guard against such temptation is to persevere. Approach each exercise slowly and without force, even gingerly at first. Be satisfied with a little progress each day (or week). Do not push yourself too soon: your body will make its own demands and decisions. If you can complete the first month, even on alternate days, you will be sufficiently convinced to continue.

The only rule, if you decide to wisely include the warm-up in your routine, is not to rest or sit down between exercises. Complete each set of repetitions as instructed, take one long deep breath, count to six, exhale slowly and continue with the next set without leaving your position. When the warm-up is finished, relax for a few moments, but keep your circulation going by walking about the room or garden. *Do not sit or lie down.* Refresh yourself with water or green tea.

DO NOT RUSH.

DO NOT OVER-EXERT.

DO NOT GIVE UP.

Loosening up:

1) Head rolling.

Relax. Stand with feet together, hands loosely at sides.

1. Roll the head slowly to the left in a clockwise direction.

2. Make sure to stretch the neck as far forward, to the side and back as possible. Complete three circles and return chin to chest.

3. Repeat three times to the right.

You may experience considerable creakings and crackings, particularly when rolling the head back over the spine, which may pop like the pulling of a knuckle joint.

It simply shows that your neck is in need of exercise and will diminish with practice.

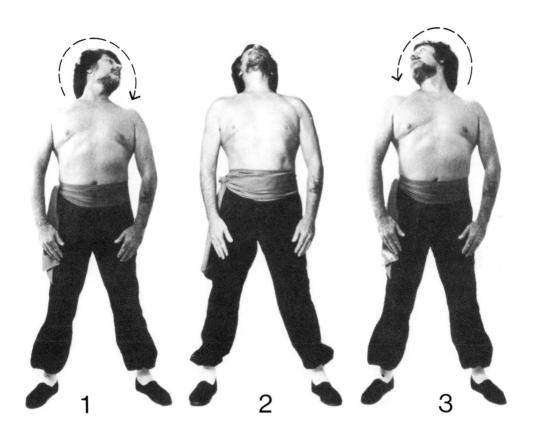

1   2   3

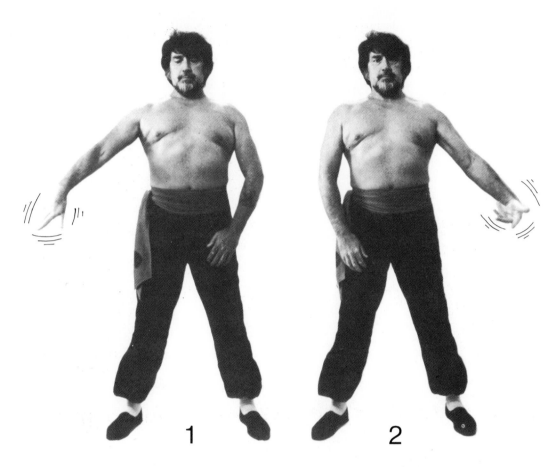

1   2

2) Finger flicking.
Relax. Stand with feet apart. Hands loosely at sides.
1. Move the right hand about 30cm away from the body and commence
to flick vigorously the loose fingers as though trying to rid them of something
sticky or to shake off drops of water. Continue for about 10 seconds or until
the whole hand is tingling with circulation.
2. Return right hand to the side and repeat with the left hand.

3) Foot shaking.

Relax. Remain standing with feet apart.

1. Lift the right foot about 15cm off the ground and commence to shake the loose foot rapidly, as though trying to kick off your shoe. Keep it up for about 10-15 seconds, keeping the leg straight, the foot shaken from the ankle not the knee, until the toes and sole tingle with circulation.

2. Repeat with the left foot.

The momentary pulsing you will experience in the palms and fingers, soles and toes is caused by a forced quickening of the blood. When shaking the foot, you may tend to lose balance. Stop and try again: you will very soon learn to retain it. The purpose of this simple opening exercise is to stimulate circulation, loosen muscles and stretch sinews, and also to relax you before beginning the warm-up.

    INHALE SLOWLY AND DEEPLY.

    HOLD FOR SILENT COUNT OF SIX.

    EXHALE SLOWLY AND STEADILY.

4) Arm circling.

To loosen and strengthen shoulders while exercising legs.

1. Open your left bow stance. Make sure the right leg is rigid and locked at the knee and that the left leg is bent well forward. Eighty per cent of the body weight is on the left leg. The left toe points to 9 o'clock. The right points to ll o'clock. The trunk should be erect from the waist up. Place the left hand in the small of the back, palm facing out.

2. Think of the right arm as a wheel and the shoulders as an axle. Commence to slowly circle the right arm forward (over-arm) as though it were a turning wheel—the shoulder is the pivot. Make sure that the arm describes a full circle on the backward swing.

3. Repeat eight times forward—arrest it in mid-swing. Reverse and swing it eight times backward (under-arm).

4. Change your stance to the left bow, and repeat the same sixteen revolutions with the left arm.

5. Return to start position with feet 45cm apart.

    INHALE SLOWLY AND DEEPLY.

    HOLD FOR COUNT OF SIX.

    EXHALE SLOWLY AND STEADILY.

Depending on the suppleness of your shoulders, you may experience a degree of popping and 'grinding' in the circling shoulder joint—plus a tendency for the circling arm to veer to the side on the backward swing as though the wheel revolves on a buckled axle. Don't straighten it by force, bend it gently to your will with patience, a little more each day until it is as easily turned backwards as it is forwards. The cracking of the shoulder ligament is to be expected if the joint is at all stiff. It will soon disappear as the shoulder becomes supple.

5) Waist twisting.

To strengthen the abdominal area and reduce the waistline while exercising the spine and back muscles. Relax.

1. Still standing with feet apart, raise the right hand above the head, palm uppermost, hand bent to a right angle from the wrist, fingers pointing left. Lower the left hand behind the back, palm down, hand bent at a right angle to the wrist, fingers pointing right.

2. Lock legs and hips to the front. Relax the trunk from the waist up. Commence twisting the upper body to the left and look behind you as far as possible. Repeat sixteen times.

3.&4. Reverse hands and repeat sixteen times to the right.

    INHALE SLOWLY AND DEEPLY.

    HOLD FOR SILENT COUNT OF SIX.

    EXHALE SLOWLY AND STEADILY.

At first, you will find a tendency to swing the hips: the pivot must be from the waist, not the hips. Concentrate on keeping the feet in position and the legs and hips locked to the front, not on how far you can turn. Waist twisting flexibility will quickly increase with practice.

1

2

3

4

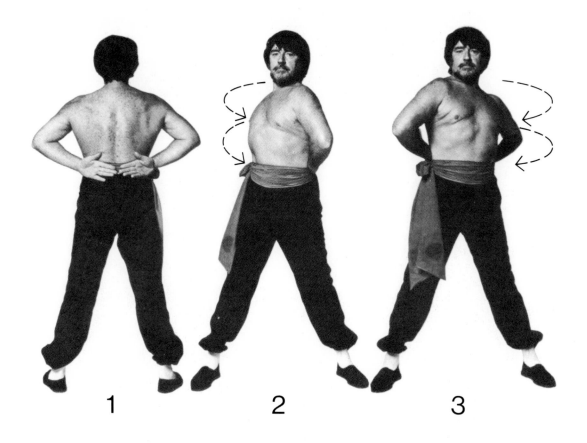

6) Shoulder blocking.

To exercise the kidney region and stomach muscles. Relax.

1. Still standing with feet apart, place the backs of the hands against the kidney area, elbows in line with shoulders.

2. Keeping this position without tension, turn the upper body as far to the left and to the right as possible, rapidly and without pause. The lower body should be kept locked to the front, the upper body pivoting from the waist only.

3. Repeat sixteen times, eight to the left and eight to the right. Return to start position.

    INHALE SLOWLY AND DEEPLY.

    HOLD FOR THE SILENT COUNT OF SIX.

    EXHALE SLOWLY AND STEADILY.

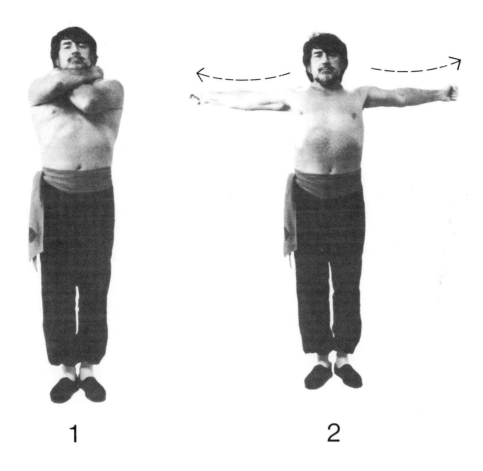

1 **2**

7) Arm flinging.

To loosen and strengthen shoulders and arms, whilst exercising the chest. Relax.

1. Draw the feet together until they are touching. Cross the forearms (left over right) under the chin with fists loosely closed.

2. Fling the arms wide, outward and back with as much force as you can muster. Make sure the out-flung arms remain at shoulder level, no higher and no lower. As the arms travel backwards, tighten your fists so that they are fully tensed at the end of the fling. Think of them as weights used to gain that extra inch to the rear. Relax the fists and arms as they return to the chest and repeat sixteen times.

    INHALE SLOWLY AND DEEPLY.

    HOLD FOR THE SILENT COUNT OF SIX.

    EXHALE SLOWLY AND STEADILY.

    You may find a tendency to lean either forward or back with the momentum of arm-flinging, also to lower the arms on the backward swing. Concentrate on remaining erect and on reaching as far to the rear as possible without lowering the arms. Go gently at first, increase the power as you feel the need.

8) Waist bending.
To exercise the back and stretch leg sinews and to increase general flexibility. Relax.
1. Still standing with feet 45cm apart, open them about another 30cm.
2. Raise the hands above the head and bring them down to touch the ground as far to the left as possible. Without fully straightening, repeat sixteen times, each time trying to reach a little further and lower to the left.
3. Straighten with hands above the head and repeat eight times to the right. Straighten to start position.
    INHALE SLOWLY AND DEEPLY.
    HOLD FOR THE SILENT COUNT OF SIX.
    EXHALE SLOWLY AND STEADILY.

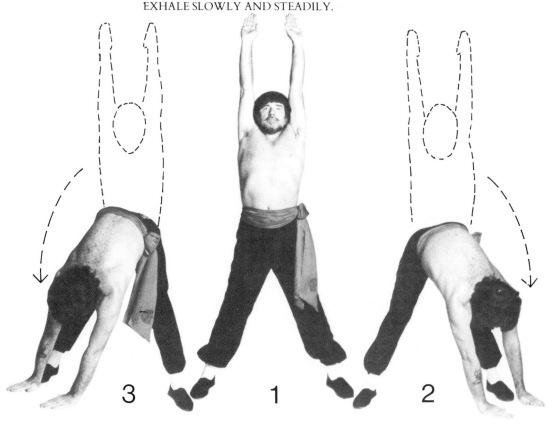

9) Seven star, chin-to-toe.
To stretch and exercise legs, back and stomach. To increase flexibility. Relax.
1. Take up the left seven star stance. Hands on hips. Bend forward along the outstretched leg as far as you can, aiming the point of the chin at the raised toe. Half rise and repeat sixteen times.
2. Reverse to the right seven star and repeat sixteen times. Straighten to start position.
    INHALE SLOWLY AND DEEPLY.
    HOLD FOR THE SILENT COUNT OF SIX.
    EXHALE SLOWLY AND STEADILY.

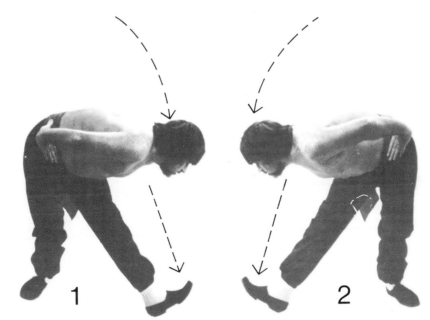

10) Seven star, nose-to-knee.

To stretch and strengthen legs and spine. To increase flexibility. This simple variation of seven star uses the foot for leverage to increase the effectiveness. Depending on your waistline, you may find a considerable distance between your nose and your knee, a gap that will close surprisingly quickly with regular practice.

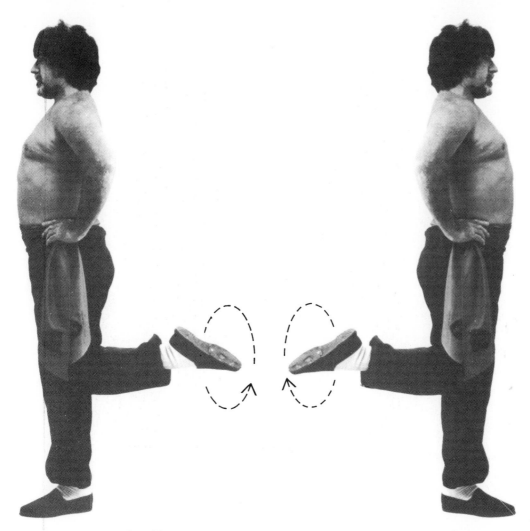

11) Ankle rotating.

To loosen and strengthen the ankles. Relax.

1. Still standing with feet together and hands on hips. Lift the left leg backwards (bent at a right angle to the knee). Rotate the foot in a circle from the ankle, eight times to the right and eight times to the left.

2. Return to the standing position, raise the right leg and repeat. Return to start position.

INHALE SLOWLY AND DEEPLY.

HOLD FOR THE SILENT COUNT OF SIX.

EXHALE SLOWLY AND STEADILY.

You may tend to lose balance and find it hard to control the circular movement of the foot: practise makes perfect.

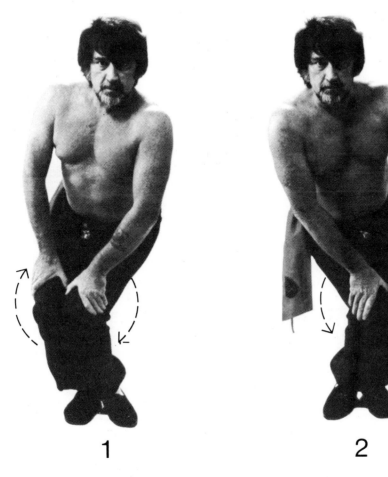

1   **2**

12) Knee rotating.
1. Stand with feet and legs close together. Bend the knees until you can grip
each leg just above the knee, while keeping the arms straight. Using that
position as a pivot, describe a deep circle around it; eight times to the right.
2. Without pausing or straightening the legs, repeat eight times to the left.
This exercise for agility may seem awkward at first but it is excellent for
loosening and strengthening the knees.

You have now completed the warm-up exercises in as little as ten minutes,
allowing for thirty second breath pauses. You have loosened the neck, arm
and leg muscles, got your circulation going, worked down to shoulders, arms,
waist, knees and ankles. Even if time does not permit these exercises to be
carried out every day, every other day or even three times a week will give
you a very nice feeling of relaxed lightness while toning you up, strengthening
and loosening taut joints and sinews. This is marvellous prelude to Pa Tuan
Tsin.

PART SIX

PA TUAN TSIN
EIGHT PRECIOUS SETS
OF EXERCISES

*"The mountain air is beautiful in
the sunset.
I drink of it as from a snow-fed
stream.
It purifies me, it strengthens me,
it calms me."*
Tao

We are now ready to begin Pa Tuan Tsin. You have chosen the spot in which you feel most natural and where the air is at its best, you are dressed in loose-fitting, comfortable clothing with ample leg room, your footwear is light and flat-bottomed, the sash around your waist is soft and not tied too tightly. You are stripped of metal accessories, your bladder and bowels are empty, you have eaten nothing for at least two hours and taken no alcohol for at least six. There is a pitcher of cool to warm boiled water or hot green tea nearby in case you need it. You remember that all inhalation and exhalation must always be through the nose, never through the mouth (unless exhalation is so instructed). All breathing should be concentrated on the slow, silent and deep. The words *patience, discipline, fortitude* and *faith* are firmly in mind.

Scoop The Stream

    The first exercise is one of the simplest and most pleasant to perform. It is so named because the second movement gives the impression of scooping water from a stream and drinking from the cupped hands.

The Benefit

It is excellent for expanding the lungs and stretching the ribcage. It also circulates the dormant Chi from the lower abdomen to the tip of the spinal column and to the forehead. It gives you a general lift and generates immediate alertness. A good way to wake up and get started.

The Execution
1. Relax. Take up your position, standing with feet together and hands loosely at sides, fix your eyes on a chosen object.
2. Empty the lungs. Inhale as slowly as you can while raising the hands (palms down) until the fingertips touch above the head (palms now up). The time required for the movement should coincide with the length of your breath. Stretch the body upward to its fullest extent without raising the heels. Imagine that you are supporting a great weight with your two palms. Hold for the silent count of three. Exhale slowly and steadily while reversing the movement and lowering the hands in time with the exhalation until they are gently back at your sides and the lungs are drained of air. Pause for the silent count of three.

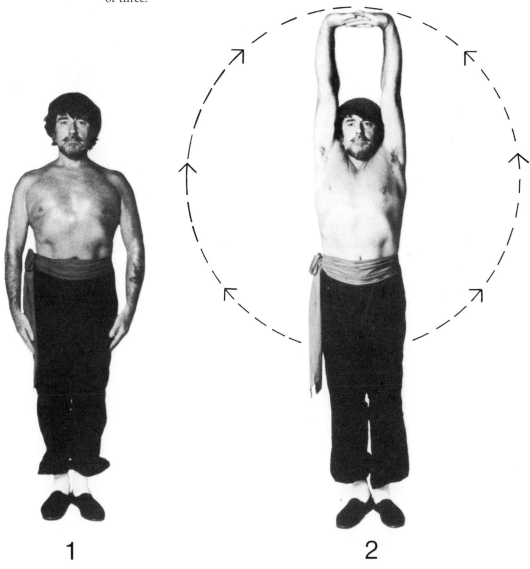

1   2

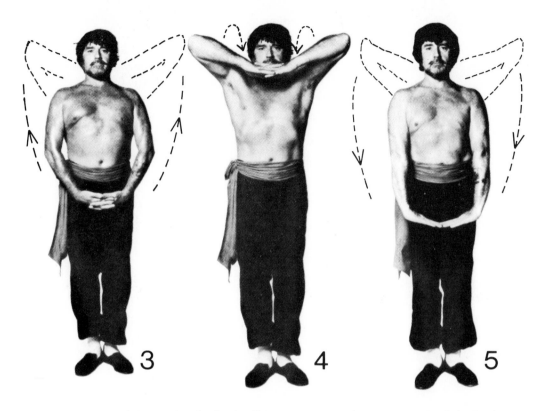

3. Intertwine the fingers, forming a scoop, palms uppermost. Inhale slowly and deeply while raising 'the scoop' to the lips, bent arms in line with shoulders, elbows raised as high as possible.

4. To the silent count of three, turn the scoop over (palms down) and exhale steadily while reversing the movement.

5. Stretch the arms downward to their fullest extent as though pressing the palms down on a spring-loaded weight. Hold for the silent count of three. Return the relaxed hands to the sides and repeat both movements eight times.

Press the Sky

The second exercise is so-called because of its ultimate stretching power. The uppermost hand and flattened palm really seem to be supporting the sky.

The Benefit

A variation of Scoop the Stream, in which the active points are the liver and the shoulders. Chi is circulated from the liver to the shoulders alternatively, conditioning the liver, stimulating its function while relieving the shoulders of strain, and stretching the entire body to its fullest extent.

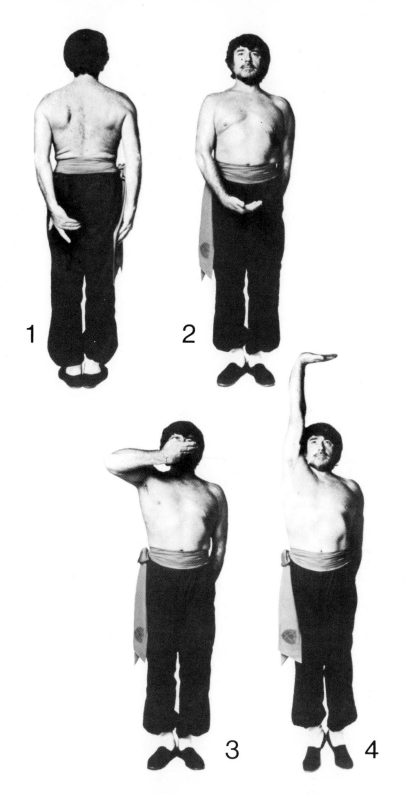

The Execution

Relax. Remain in position with feet together.

1. Reach behind with the left hand and firmly clasp the back of the thigh, just below the left buttock.

2. Drain the lungs of air. Form a 'cup' with the right hand hooked at the wrist.

3. Inhale slowly and deeply while raising the cup to the lips, elbow in line with shoulder.

4. Without pause, turn the cup outward and over, rise on your toes and continue inhaling until the right arm is 'pressing the sky'. From toes to upturned palm, your body is stretched to its absolute utmost and full of air. Hold for the count of three.

5., 6. & 7. Exhale slowly and steadily and reverse the action exactly: lower the upturned palm to the lips while lowering the heels. Form the cup at the lips, lower to the groin, relax with both hands at the sides. Reach behind with the right hand to grasp the right back thigh below the buttock. Repeat the movements exactly with the left hand. Complete four times with each arm.

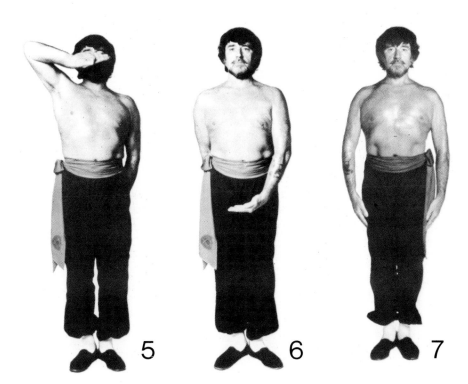

The Shaolin Archer

The third and much-revered exercise is perhaps the most 'beautiful jewel in the crown of the Precious Eight' . . . at least that is how it was once described by a Shaolin priest. Its quite classical performance is reminiscent of a Chinese opera, where all sets, props and even weapons are imaginary. It is best described as the drawing of a longbow hewn from the oldest yew or blackwood or forged of the finest steel. It is a bow that takes the strength, artistry and skill of the true archer to bend.

The Benefit

This exercise can be used alone when time does not permit the full sequence, it being considered the most beneficial of the set. Its primary purpose, because of its separate (left and right) stretching, is to exercise alternate lung power. At the same time its twisting motion under pressure relieves and strengthens the liver. Executed from the Half-horse (or full Horse, if you feel like it), it also brings into play the leg, hip and spinal exercise explained under Horse Stance, plus the stretching and strengthening of sinew and joint in the arm, developing unexpected power.

The Execution

Relax. Drop into a Half-horse Stance (high-seated, knees half-bent). Settle comfortably, checking your stance for perfect balance; move your foot a centimetre or two to find it.

1. Take a long, silent breath while raising the right arm and holding it at shoulder level. The left hand is on the left thigh. The right hand is relaxed from the wrist, the right arm firm but not tensed. Keep your eyes, half-closed, upon the outstretched hand. Think of nothing else but the hand. It is a beautiful thing. It is your hand, it has accompanied you and obeyed you throughout your life. It has many times saved you, it is your closest friend, without it you are lost. Love your precious hand as it moves to your will.

2. Swing the hand in its gentle state slowly across your body just below eye-level, keeping the arm locked but relaxed. Watch its progress as though it were a bird in flight, until it is across your chest and pointing left. During this flight, you are gently exhaling, emptying your lungs quietly but completely.

3. Before it has finished travelling, bring up the bow (left hand). Your lungs are now empty and ready to draw breath. Raise the forefinger of the left hand as though its tip were a target (or a gun sight).

4. Inhale slowly, quietly, steadily, as you push out the bow to full arm's length, keeping your eyes fixed on the raised finger tip. Straighten the left arm to its fullest extent, locking the elbow until the full breath has been drawn. At the same time, the 'arrow hand' has been slowly drawn back to its fullest extent. All motion should cease with the peak of your inhalation. In other words, your movements last as long as your slowest inhalation and exhalation.

Hold the pose for the silent count of three. During that period of three seconds, with lungs fully extended, concentrate through willpower your entire bodily strength into your raised fingertip. Stretch that extended right arm to its absolute maximum and a little bit more. The elbow and wrist should tighten like a stretched rope, just the way a cat puts every ounce of power into the awakening stretch of its forelegs.

5. On three, begin to gently exhale and repeat the exact procedure in reverse, lowering the right hand slowly to the thigh and now relaxing the taut left hand at the wrist.

6., 7. & 8. The left hand has now become the arrow hand and the right will raise the bow. Exhale as the left hand swings slowly into position and draw the bow to the right.

This may sound complicated but you will find that it is not. Just imagine the fitting, drawing and releasing of an imaginary bow, drawn first to the right and then to the left. Repeat four times on either side.

Search the Clouds

The fourth exercise is referred to in Wu Shu circles as 'a very essential health dose'. This may be an added incentive to practise it correctly as it appears quite awkward to perform and calls for considerable physical application. It is called Search the Clouds because the movements command attention upwards.

The Benefit

Its benefit can be seen after internal injuries such as bruises or contusion caused from heavy sparring or actual combat. This indicates its internal effectiveness. It is also accepted as a pick-up for fatigue and over-exertion 'especially after sexual intimacy'. Sexual exhaustion or tiredness can interfere with bodily functions, in particular the digestive system. Searching the clouds hardly seems a recuperative procedure for a bruised or weary body, but with careful and regular practice you will find that it is.

The Execution

Relax. Remain in the Half-horse Stance (or rest your legs for a moment if you must), then lower into the full Horse Stance.

1. Place the hands on the thighs, fingers spread inwards.

2. Slowly inhale, while bending the upper body backwards and to the left as far as you can go. The lungs and body should be filled with air by the time you have reached the full extent of your backward bend.

3. Hold for the silent count of three, pressing back to gain another centimetre. Exhale steadily as you bring the upper body forward to its central position, by which time the lungs and body are drained of air.

Relax. Hold for the silent count of three.

4. Repeat the movement to the right. Complete four times on each side. Close the Horse Stance and stand erect.

Lift the Rock

The fifth exercise is a combination of exercises one and two: scooping and pressing. The basic movement is that of taking the weight of a rock or nearby object in the hands, lifting it to the chin and raising it as high above the head as possible.

The Benefit

It offers all-round internal benefits while bringing about the utmost in upward stretching. We have all observed the animal stretching habits, particularly feline, upon waking or rising. No authority on physical energy control and bodily relaxation could deny that stretching has considerable restorative effects.

The Execution

1. Relax. Stand erect with feet together. Empty the lungs of air.

2. Entwine the fingers, palms uppermost (to accept the rock).

3. Inhale slowly and deeply while raising the joined hands level with the chin.

4. Continue the upward press without breaking the finger grip, turning the palms outward and upward as you continue to press above the head. Follow the movement of your hands with your eyes until your flat, upturned palms have reached their utmost height. Strain to gain an extra fraction, to the silent count of three. Relax.

5. Exhale steadily while reversing the movement exactly.

6. Back to the beginning position. Press down for the silent count of three. Repeat eight times.

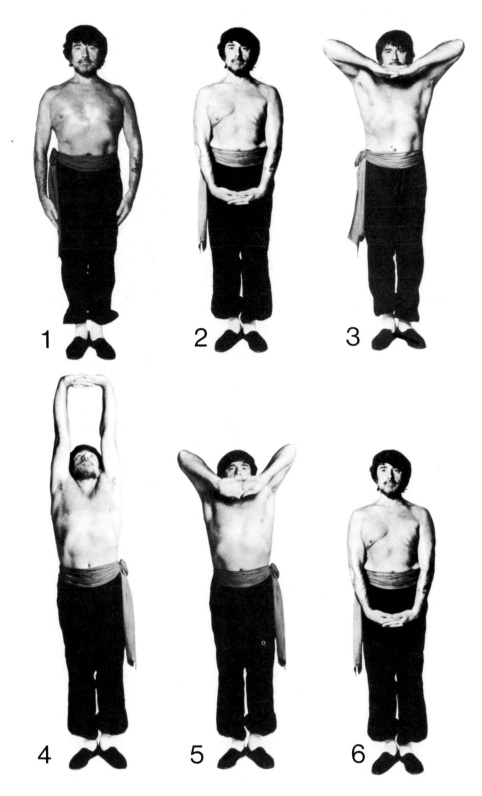

1   2   3

4   5   6

Touch the Sky
Press the Earth

The sixth exercise combines maximum upward stretching with maximum forward and downward stretching, hence the name.

The Benefit

Maximum stretching and bending combines arm and shoulder loosening, chest expansion, abdominal, back and leg exercise whilst greatly benefiting the kidneys and spleen.

The Execution

1. Relax. Stand erect with feet together, hands loose at sides. Empty the lungs of air.

2. Inhale slowly and deeply while raising the hands above the head and continuing a backward bend as far as possible. Hold for the silent count of three.

3. Exhale steadily while reversing the movement forward and down until the fingertips are pressed on the ground as far ahead of your toes as possible. Pause for the silent count of five.

4. Inhale slowly and deeply while straightening, drawing the hands up the legs to the thighs.

5. Hold for the silent count of three.

6. Repeat eight times.

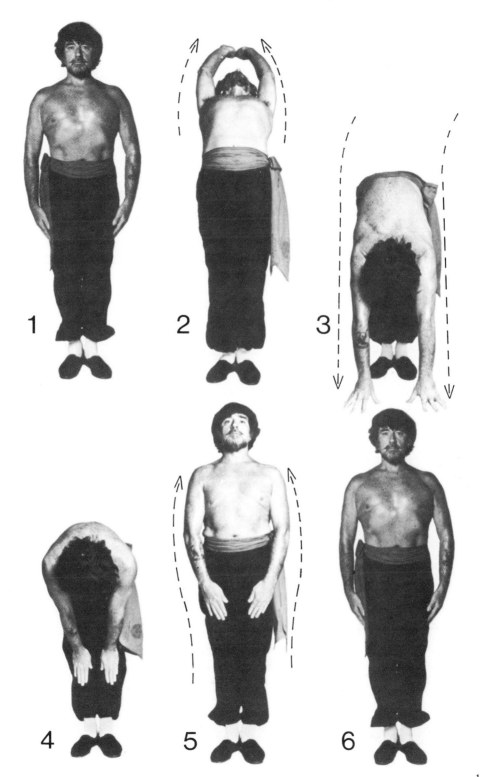

1   2   3

4   5   6

113

Eye of the Tiger

The seventh exercise is perhaps so named because of the tiger's ability to look directly behind it while keeping its body poised for a frontal spring. We have all seen a cat stalking some unsuspecting prey, only to be disturbed by a sound or movement behind it. It will stop dead in its tracks, front paw raised, every muscle and sinew frozen in the direction of its chosen path, while turning its head to look directly back over its tail. Apparently tigers do this also.

The Benefit

Whatever the origin of its name, this seems as good an explanation as any, for it is just this action that the exercise calls for. It loosens neck sinews, develops neck muscles, exercises the vital organs of the throat and promotes excellent balance while working calves, ankles and feet.

The Execution

1. Relax. Stand erect with feet together, hands loose at sides. Empty the lungs of air.

2. Inhale slowly and deeply while gradually rising on the toes and turning the head as far to the left as possible. Do not turn the shoulders or upper body.

When the breath is complete, you should be fully raised on the toes, head twisted as far to the left as possible in an attempt to look behind you. Hold for the silent count of three.

3. Exhale steadily while reversing the movement back to the starting position.

4. Repeat movement to the right. Complete four times on either side.

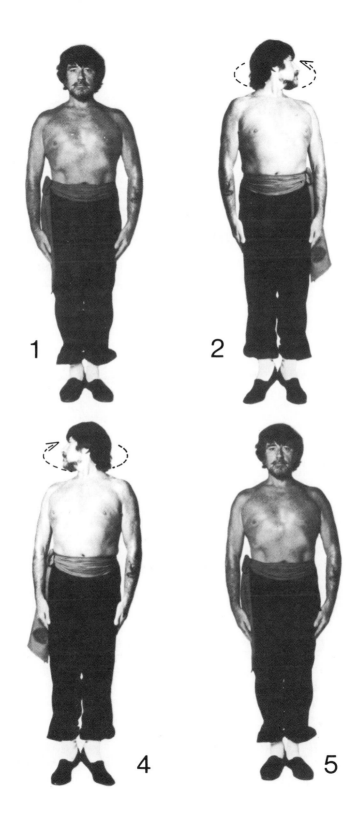

Grip the Swallow's Egg

The name of this eighth exercise is derived from the unique way of closing the fists. Each fist is fully formed yet leaves a hollow in its centre as though protecting a delicate object from being crushed. The fist, tensed to its full power when outstretched, must control the energy that surrounds the inner palm. This exercise develops a formidable hand grip, greatly strengthens the arm while demanding passive control. It is one of the classic restraining movements, which, when released with full speed and impact after long practice, can unleash unbelievable but easily controlled force.

The Benefit

To increase power in the arms, from shoulder to elbow, to wrist, to fingers, is the main purpose; at the same time exercising the legs and lower trunk. It is in fact the 'slow motion' performance of the 'Kung Fu' punch with strict control on pressure and the restraint of energy. It is a little difficult to master and should be practised patiently and diligently from one stance at a time until ready to progress to the next. Pa Tuan Tsin only teaches the frontal punch, but I have included punching from the Right and Left Bow.

The Execution

1. Relax. From the Horse Stance, empty the lungs of air.

2. Inhale slowly and deeply while extending the right fist in a frontal punch. The movement should begin from a relaxed shoulder, gradually increasing pressure as it turns and extends. When the fist is fully extended (imaginary swallow's egg safely shielded inside), tensed as if in a strike, the arm is also locked at the elbow, exerting full pressure. Hold for the silent count of three.

3. Exhale steadily as you reverse the movement, withdrawing the fist and slackening pressure as it returns to the waist and complete relaxation. Hold for the silent count of three.

4. Repeat the movement with the left fist. Repeat eight times.

5. & 6. Without rising from the Horse Stance, twist into the Left Bow position and repeat the exact movement, aiming the restrained punch at an imaginary target on your right. Four punches with each arm.

7. & 8. Twist into the Right Bow position and repeat two punches to the left.

Close the Horse Stance, stand erect. Relax and lower the hands to the sides. Inhale. Exhale.

9

9. Bow to the light that is in you.

The final exercise of the Precious Eight may leave you a little wobbly
at the knees, but otherwise feeling fine once you have closed the Horse Stance
and straightened up. The temptation to sit down will also be great. Resist
it. Ease tired leg muscles by walking about or, if you are practising in a
room, just walking on the spot. Keep your legs moving for at least a five
minute period.

Sip some water or tea, allow your breathing to settle and become completely
normal.

Now that the Eight Precious Sets of Exercises have been demonstrated there should be a few words about getting the maximum benefit out of your practice in the shortest time.

As with any routine, there will be those who make faster progress than others; some that are fitter or younger to begin with and take to it more naturally, and those who will find it more difficult to adapt to. The biggest danger, especially when learning from the words and pictures of a book without coaching or encouragement, is 'faith-lag', that drop in confidence in oneself and in the exercises that is bound to occur during the early stages of a forced discipline overseen by no-one but yourself. How do we avoid the temptation to drop out? To start with, you would not have read this far unless you felt an interest or a need for some kind of improvement in your health. But that doesn't mean you will consider the contents without a certain amount of reservation.

As I have stressed at every opportunity, patience, discipline and willpower are the vital ingredients. Unlike many advertised 'get-fit' systems, these breathing exercises do not carry a money-back guarantee of a magnificent body in only seven days for just five minutes a day. They do not promise effortless, easy results that will neither interfere with your life nor take up your time. But, I repeat, they do offer at the very least definite, self-evident improvement in general fitness, increased strength and a degree of immunity from illness which might otherwise affect a less healthy body.

The various benefits to be had from Pa Tuan Tsin and the time taken to achieve them is entirely up to you, as is the ultimate goal of Chi. There is, however, a yardstick by which you can judge your progress and this also works as a guard against 'faith-lag'. Assuming you are able to adopt a daily routine (or at second best, every other day), the first four weeks will undoubtedly prove to be the dropping out period. You are very likely to find many of the exercises awkward and uncomfortable to execute in the beginning. Or, on the other hand, they may seem so easy that you will consider them meaningless. There will almost certainly be days when the last thing you will wish to contemplate is yourself in a pair of droopy pyjamas, poised unsteadily before a mirror, confronted by a neighbour's fence or a panorama of city roof-tops; not to mention miserable weather and the possible indignities of a giggle or two from sceptical members of the household.

You will almost certainly find breath and body co-ordination difficult during the first few sessions. The combination of your mind, breathing and body movements may seem totally out of reach. That first month is the testing ground; the proving period that you must come through no matter how slowly, before you realise that you have begun.

It is best, then, to be aware of the normal stumbling blocks you can expect to encounter and how to deal with them. Firstly, do not hurry in your efforts to immediately follow the routine as laid out. It has been made clear that the warm-up exercises and extra exercises are not an essential part of the programme, you may wish to leave them until you feel you want to include them.

You may even find it disheartening to try to follow the exact sequence of the exercises. Don't then. Study the stance and posture of each exercise separately, get familiar with the feel of different movements and positions before attempting to co-ordinate them with your breathing. If a particular muscle or joint seems stubborn at a certain angle, be patient with it, massage it, coax it into position, test it tolerantly and be satisfied with the response until you feel it is ready for extra demands. You will very soon discover your body's capabilities and develop your own style.

Likewise with your breathing. As suggested earlier, practise it separately, concentrating first on prolonging and controlling the length and depth of your inhalation and exhalation by deep breathing as often as you can. Practise by-passing the lungs and reaching the diaphragm before applying breathing to body movement. Remember breathing can be practised at any time; in the car, walking the dog, at the office window, in bed or in the bath. You are always breathing, so why not practise breathing properly? Slowly and deeply through the nose.

You cannot always choose or influence the quality of the air you breathe and, of course, there are times and places when the shorter and shallower your respiration the better; in the wake of a diesel engine, for instance, in a particularly smoky bar or any closed-in and crowded area. But most of the time there is nothing like slow, deep breathing to calm the nerves and liven up the step. More about the quality of air later on.

You will know when your breathing is improved, not only by its duration and depth but by its passage. You will find it cooling the back of your throat like a subdued rush of cold breeze rather than a scarcely noticed rhythm in the nostrils; your diaphragm will rise and fall rather than your chest and ribcage. This fresh awareness of breath is the first foothold in the climb to Chi and assures you that you are ready to apply it to Pa Tuan Tsin.

One last but very important word. Should you have any doubts whatever as to your physical capability to perform any of the exercises or should you find any one particularly difficult, it would be wise to take this book along to your doctor and ask his opinion. This is particularly advisable if you are in poor health or suffering from any specific complaint.

If you decide that some of the exercises are not possible for you or just don't seem right, then drop them out of the sequence until you feel ready for them, adding them as you make progress or leaving them out all together.

The wonderful thing about Pa Tuan Tsin is that even if you were to practise only one of the exercises continually you would soon feel the benefit. Older Chinese, for instance, often have a favourite exercise and they practise it and nothing else every morning. The Shaolin Archer is one such gem. All over Hong Kong or any Chinese area in Asia you will see amahs and coolies, businessmen and shopkeepers, all drawing their imaginary bows in the first soft light of moring. Their Horse Stance may vary greatly in height and style, but they are all enjoying the same air.

An effective summary of the Chinese attitudes towards progress is contained in the following extract from my first Chin Wu examination report:

The perfection of your art lies in the difficult region between the heart's intent and the expression of this intent in gesture. You know as well as we do where your problem is: in hesitation, in the lack of confidence in your stances and movements. Perhaps your will to learn has surged ahead of your body's capacity to understand the lessons of the dances. You should learn to relax, to be kind and patient to your own body. Practise your forms in peace. You have done better than you think.

PART SEVEN

EXTRA EXERCISES

"Breath is the Emperor and the
mind is the Prime Minister.
Breath is active in sleep,
whereas the mind is not."
Hindu saying.

The following exercises are not a part of Pa Tuan Tsin but they are recommended for those who can find the time and stamina to fit them in. Perhaps begin to include them as you become further advanced. Each of them is part of the Wu Shu exercise routine and designed to improve the circulation of Chi. They are not so much breathing exercises but rather exercises for strengthening the legs, arms and hands.

Leg Stretching.

Firstly, the simple process of stretching the legs and bending at the waist, in much the same way as a ballet dancer will practise on a wall bar. If you don't have a bar, the garden fence or an improvisation will do.
The Execution

Start with the bar at a comfortable (but not too comfortable) height — at least waist high. Raise the right leg until the heel is resting upon the bar with the leg absolutely straight. Left leg rigid, locked at the knee, toe at 12 o'clock.
1. Reach forward and grasp the right foot with the right hand, pressing down on the knee with the left.
2. Using the right toe as leverage, bring the nose as close to the knee as possible.
Repeat as many times as you can, building up to twenty and then to forty as soon as you are able. Reverse position and repeat with left leg.

This exercise really puts the muscles and tendons in the backs of the legs to work. Don't be surprised or concerned if you experience soreness, it will soon disappear. Leg stretching will also help you in the bending exercises of Pa Tuan Tsin.

Squatting.

After a session of leg stretching, the overwhelming urge is to bend them. Simple squats executed slowly bring instant relief to stretched legs and complete the natural movement.

The Excution

1. Stand erect with feet together. Rise on toes. Inhale slowly and deeply. Exhale steadily while squatting as slowly as possible, raising the arms to the sides.

2. Do not lower your weight onto your heels. At the end of the breath, you should be squatting with knees three-quarters bent and arms outstretched, level with shoulders. Hold for the silent count of three.

Reverse the movement by slowly rising and lowering the arms while inhaling slowly and deeply on the way up. Repeat as many times as comfortable (try for five and increase with progress).

Kicking Shadows

Apart from the striking power developed by such leg exercises, Kicking Shadows is a very effective way to try out these new legs of yours. And after six weeks of practising the Horse Stance, you will indeed have new legs.

There are many kicks for the Wu Shu practitioner to develop: side, back and front, performed from standing, squatting, lying, or from mid-air, often a good two metres above the ground. These highly dangerous and difficult lightning strikes with the feet are perhaps the most breathtaking and incredible manifestations of the power of Chi in the advanced Wu Shu student. They are far beyond the reach of the average healthy and athletic man and, of course, are best left alone by all but the serious martial artist.

I have chosen the two most simple but effective strike kicks, emphasising that they are suggested as an excellent addition to your Pa Tuan Tsin practice. They are offered only to speed up the reflexes and to test and increase leg power. They are also an excellent way of letting off steam when the spirit of Chi is at its height.

It must be emphasised that their use as a strike, even in defence, should be avoided at all costs unless you are under the supervision of a recognised Kung Fu instructor. Even then he will advise against their use unless in deadly combat. Frontal kicks, both high and low (throat/chest, groin/knee) can not only cause serious injury or death, they can also put the kicker at a total balance disadvantage unless he is an expert.

The Low Snap Kick.

1. Feet together, knees slightly bent, hands firmly in punch position. Inhale.
2. Raise the left knee and snap the foot out from the waist with a whip-like action, making sure the striking foot is stretched in line with the leg.

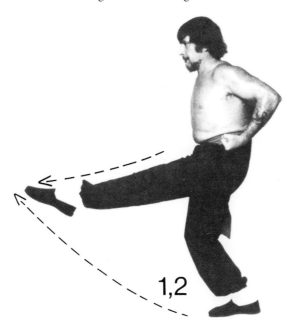

1,2

3   4

The High Snap Kick.
3. From the Right Bow Stance, raise the left hand, open palm down, arm
straight from the shoulder. Inhale.
4. Bend the left leg at the knee and snap it out to strike the raised palm
with the outstretched foot. As soon as the strike is made, return the leg to
its Bow Position. Speed, power and stability are the purpose; accuracy of aim
and contact will come with practice. As you progress, repeat the low kick
as many times as you are able (aim for ten). Reverse to the Left Bow and
repeat with the right foot. This is, of course, more difficult to perform, perhaps
impossible, if you are not including leg stretching in your routine.

Note. You may find either of these kicking techniques difficult to cultivate
as demonstrated and if so dispense with the Bow position and the target
of the hand. Simply practise the kicks from the standing punch position with
knees half-bent until you have developed the balance and the knack.

Bend like the Grass

An exercise in agility and flexibility, this and similar classic postures are widely used in several forms of Wu Shu. Basically a feinting manoeuvre, it leaves an opponent with the impression of retreat while actually avoiding a leg attack or dodging a fist strike and positioning for an unexpectedly low counter attack.

For our purpose, however, it is merely a satisfying culmination for all your patient leg work. It may take you some time to achieve it comfortably and steadily, but achieve it you will. It is perhaps the ultimate leg exercise when all other work has prepared you for it.

The Execution

1. Take up the left Seven Star position. Raise the hands as though warding off a blow to the chest.

2. Sink back on the right bent knee, toe at 1 o'clock, until all weight is taken by the fully bent right leg. Keep the back straight and upright.

3 **4**

3. With the left hand placed just above the left knee, press down hard as if trying to force the leg to touch the ground. Repeat as many times as possible (try for twenty).

4. Change the foot to a side angle, toe at 2 o'clock, sole and heel flat to the ground, reverse the angle of the hand and repeat another twenty times. Without standing or shifting the position of the feet, reverse the position so that the right leg is outstretched and all weight upon the fully-bent left leg and repeat **(5, 6, 7).**

This is a difficult manoeuvre for anyone whose hips and lower joints are unaccustomed to regular exercises and it should only be attempted in the sixth week of practice. It is likely that at first you will lose balance, find yourself unable to 'get down' all the way and feel far from dignified. You will discover though, that you can get a little lower, a little more stable, upright and comfortable each day, until it is a pleasure to reach and hold with ease. A quiet conclusion to your months of patience, determination and discipline.

5

6

7

Move The Mountain

Move the Mountain is a classic Tiger Claw exercise. Although somewhat modified for our purpose, it develops power in the arms and shoulders while giving the benefit of the Horse Stance, increasing lung capacity and improving circulation. The Chinese believe this exercise has excellent recuperative effects and use it to round off a heavy training session or to wind down after a bout of free sparring. It is an ideal way to complete your practice.

The Execution

1. Open the Horse Stance.

2. Inhale fully, bringing the arms up and elbows back until the hands are beside the shoulders, palms facing out and forefingers pointing up.

3. Exhale slowly and steadily as the hands are very gradually pushed forward in line with the knees. Force is concentrated along the arms to the fingertips as though rolling a boulder from the mouth of a cave that imprisons you.

At the end of the breath every ounce of strength and mental concentration should be directed to the fingertips, arms stretched to their fullest and held for the count of three.

Exhale slowly and steadily while relaxing the arms and withdrawing them back to the shoulder position. Hold for the count of three and repeat eight times.

1

2

3

Palm, Fist and Finger Press-ups

That good old-fashioned stand-by, the body press-up, has been a popular part of physical culture since man recognised the need to stay strong. It is the natural effort of pitting your strength and the weight of your body against gravity.

The palm, fist and finger press-ups are no different except for slight refinements designed to strengthen hand power. They are as optional as the leg stretching exercises and only offered for those energetic enough to continue after Pa Tuan Tsin.

Most of us have performed press-ups at some time or other: at school, in training for sport, in the gym or in the forces. Yet this comparatively ordinary exercise is so often executed wrongly. To get the most out of press-ups, the back *must* be kept straight, not raised at the behind to ease weight **(1)**. Arm muscles are most benefited if the hands are turned inwards and the feet are higher than the head, to increase weight upon the arms and upper body **(2)**.

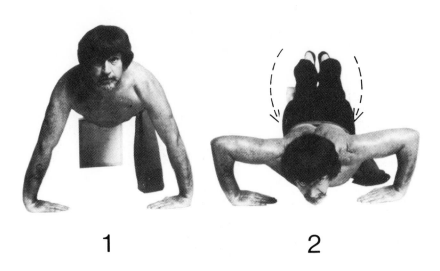

1   2

Breathing correctly while executing push-ups is also very important, yet seldom understood. Most often the habit is to lock the larynx and use breath stored in the body to push against. This is incorrect and burdens the heart with excessive effort. The up movement should be used for inhalation and the down movement for exhalation.

Another chest development method is to do your press-ups between three chairs **(5, 6).** This is not recommended until at least forty normal press-ups

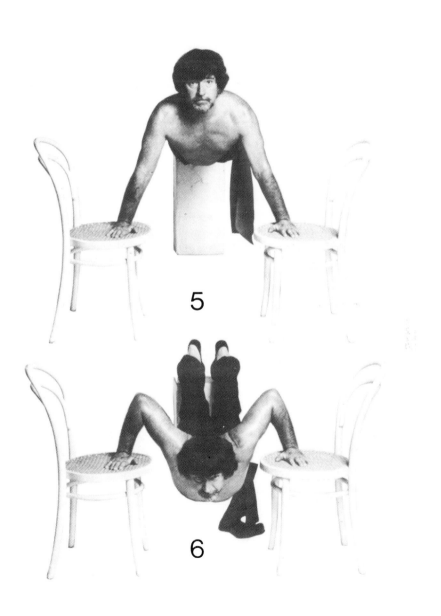

5

6

are part of your everyday routine.

The variation of press-ups performed on the knuckles of the closed fist **(3)** may seem a little unnecessary, and to some perhaps it is. Its purpose (apart from hardening the fists and strengthening the wrists) is to promote discipline through a little harmless endurance. Taking the weight of one's body squarely upon the knuckles is hardly a comfortable sensation at first, but once tried, even one or two repetitions at a time and gradually increased, it will have a marked effect upon your confidence when relying on your hands. It does not ruin or deform hands, although you may at first develop slight knuckle callouses, especially if you have practised on concrete or some other rough surface.

Finger press-ups are devised to fortify the fingers **(4).** They should be attempted after fist press-ups have become natural and simple to perform twenty-five to fifty times (which may take six months to a year of daily practice). Even then, they should be built up with utmost caution so as not to strain the hand.

The Chinese have a favourite story to demonstrate the business of over-exercising the fingers. It tells of a woodcutter who set about developing the strongest hands in the forest so that he might wield the heaviest axe and fell twice the number of trees in half the time, thereby bringing prosperity to his poor family.

He disappeared into the woods and for a whole year practised finger press-ups until he could pick up a cooking wok by its convex bottom with his finger and thumb. He then proudly went home to break the news. He knocked on the door, removing it from its hinges, slapped his son on the back, knocking the life out of him, took his wife's hand in sorrow and broke it, and when blowing his nose in remorse, it came away in his handkerchief.

Although a little far-fetched and a trifle violent, at least this tale demonstrates the caution with which excessive power of the hands should be utilised. We will not go on to one finger press-ups for the simple reason that I cannot perform them — my one and only effort put me out of action for a month!

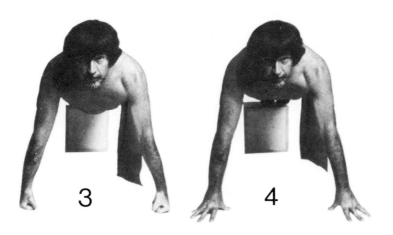

PART EIGHT

MEDITATION
AND CHI

*'There are but three ways:
the way of the Heavens,
the way of the Earth,
and the way we must follow,
the Tao'*
Lin Tui

Meditation and Chi

Most forms of physical discipline practised in Asia have a strong connection with meditation. The further one goes into the study of self-mastery, the more important control of the mind becomes. A Chinese saying sums it up: 'In order to tame the horse you must first control the rider'. No great Master of the past reached his ultimate goal without bringing his thoughts and emotions to heel. They believed that if the untrained body were as erratic in its movements as the untrained mind, a man would be lucky to come through a day of his life unscathed — not an exaggeration when we consider the tangents our minds so often take without rhyme or reason and think of the consequences if our bodies behaved in a similar way. Most of us would be lucky to get from one side of the road to the other, let alone survive behind the wheel of a car.

So, the great Masters believed a trained body was impossible without a trained mind. In this sense meditation was used to store and release energy at will, to conserve Chi and to unleash it with speed and power. This phenomenon is illustrated in its purest form by the almost superhuman feats demonstrated by the advanced external, or 'hard style', martial artist. The shattering of bricks and roof tiles, piercing of boards and buckling of metal with the foot or fist are not tricks. They are achieved by total concentration of mind, body and breath, concentrated upon the single spot and the single thought until nothing else exists in the universe except the strike. The often terrifying sound that accompanies such great effort is caused by the sudden release of breath rather than a will to impress onlookers. This harnessing of power is far too violent for our simple purpose of improved breathing.

Although, related to breath control and the development of Chi, meditation is also relevant to Pa Tuan Tsin. Any effective fitness routine calls for total concentration. It is utterly useless to approach a half hour of relaxing exercise with a racing mind that cannot be stilled.

Various kinds of meditation are nowadays prescribed as readily as enemas and emetics. Unfortunately, relief through meditation is not so easily achieved. In recent decades, encouraged by Western interest in oriental religions and philosophies, gurus, some qualified and some not, have been flourishing by pointing out the many pathways leading to the inner light. A few of them, mostly Indian and vastly experienced in the ways of yoga, are recognised as Masters of Prana, the yogic equivalent of Chi, the life-force to be drawn from the air around us. Charles Johnston, in his translation of *The Yoga Sutras of Patanjali, the Book of the Spiritual Man* (Stuart & Watkins, London, 1970), clearly describes the three limbs of yoga: concentration, meditation and contemplation:

'The binding of the perceiving consciousness to a certain region is attention (concentration); *a holding of the perceiving consciousness in that region is meditation; when the perceiving consciousness in this meditation is wholly given to illuminating the essential meaning of the object contemplated and is freed from the sense of separateness and personality, this is contemplation.'*

It is a great pity that meditation and, in fact, most forms of spiritual reflection are so unattainable to the average person who is in greatest need yet furthest from its fulfilment. Successful meditation is probably the most elusive of all 'self-help' methods. In spite of the countless volumes, increasing interest, qualified classes and courses, it remains a mystery far too complex to be learnt from the pages of a book.

And yet, you can walk into any health store or bookshop today and spend an indecisive hour searching through scores of titles on meditation and every other aspect of human improvement. Think of something you don't know about healthy, happy living and you'll find it on the rack. How to bring up your kids, how to tolerate your parents, how to make love, masturbate, increase your libido, grow new hair, face ageing and death with dignity, sleep soundly, relax and stop yourself from going crazy.

Much of the information is concerned with how to challenge and overcome the demon, stress. Anxiety and fear, resulting in depression and perhaps serious mental illness, have become as everyday and hard to cure as the common cold or bunion. Billions of dollars are spent each year on millions of multi-coloured capsules containing temporary relief from the effects of daily doses of stress. Some of them help but none of them cure. And so, meditation in its many forms, both physic and mystic, has finally found its way from the past of the East and taken a prominent place in the present and future of the West.

As serious and difficult as the search for religious faith, meditation is perhaps the most elusive of all pursuits leading towards peace of mind. Its results are the hardest of all to achieve and will only come to the serious student through discipline and self-control far beyond the ordinary.

In spite of generous men like Yogi Ramacharaka, Patanjali and others, the true gurus of the inner self do not give away their knowledge lightly. Most of the information available is either a second hand version from a Western enthusiast or the work of a renegade sensationalist from the Orient out to make a name for himself. Fame and fortune have no place in true meditation. It is only the rare oracle, dedicated to the selfless elevation of the mortal soul, who is qualified to teach another human being to meditate upon life and his or her place in it.

Does meditation have a place in the practice of Pa Tuan Tsin? Yes it does. Simple initiation to forms of mind relaxation are taught in the second year at Chin Wu. It is stressed that progressive stages are only introduced to the advanced student and even then with great care and consideration. Masters of Chin Wu believe that indiscriminate dabbling can not only have the opposite effect to quietude, but may prove harmful. They go out of their way to lead into it with the utmost care, encouraging certain minds while gently suggesting infinite patience to others. After all, they say 'a bamboo

door can believe it is a wooden door and never know the truth', which
is a way of saying 'you don't *have* to come to terms with yourself . . . millions
don't and manage to get through life quite well'.

Any serious programme of health improvement in today's anxiety-stricken
environment would seem inadequate without at least a mention of meditation.
It is far too complex a subject to be dealt with by anyone but the few great
experts of the major mystical schools of Yoga, Zen, Sufism and Gurdjieff.
Books such as *The New Religions* by Jacob Needleman (Doubleday, New
York, 1970); Huston Smith's *Religions of Man* (Harper and Row, New York,
1958); and, for a Western philosophy of meditation, Evelyn Underhill's
Mysticism (E.P. Dutton, New York, 1961) will give the serious seeker a great
deal to contemplate.

Contrary to many casual interpretations of meditation, it is not intended
as a means of escaping reality or dulling the awareness of things that you
would prefer to ignore or forget. It is an often difficult but always rewarding
attempt to train and tune the mind, much as an athlete masters and disciplines
his body. The end result of successful meditation is to increase one's awareness
rather than diminish it and to transcend the painful and negative aspects
of everyday life with serenity and greater efficiency.

Saint Theresa of Avila is said to have likened the human mind to an
'unbroken horse that would go anywhere except where you wanted it to'.
Plato had a very original answer to the problems of a mind adrift. He
compared it to a sailing ship commanded by a mutinous crew. With the
true captain and his navigator safely in irons, the 'free' sailors take turns in
steering the ship without knowledge or direction, foundering on the rocks
or being hopelessly lost in strange oceans. Man's quest, he said, was to quell
the mutiny, release the captain and navigator, plot a fresh but definite course
and stay on it until the ultimate destination is reached.

A similar analogy is shown in these lines from a Sanskrit poem written
in India between the second and fifth centuries BC:

> The wind turns a ship from its course upon the waters.
> The wandering winds of the senses cast man's mind adrift,
> and turn his better judgement from its courses.
> When a man can still his senses I call him illumined.

Such pearls of wisdom are all very well, you may say, but how do I attain
it? Where do I begin? One effective way of testing your powers of
concentration is in 'counting your breath'. It may sound absurdly simple,
but after trying it for fifteen minutes we realise how right Saint Theresa
was and how close to the mark Plato's ship is sailing.

To find out for yourself, just stand, sit or lie in a comfortable position,
in a spot with as little distraction as possible, and remain still. Begin counting
each steady inhalation from one to eight and then begin again at one and
so on for up to fifteen minutes. If nothing more, the exercise will give you
an inkling of what it feels like to meditate and it will almost certainly alarm
you to find how undisciplined your thoughts really are. That horse will be
away, over fences with the bit in its mouth!

Although enough books and self-styled experts are available on the practices
and philosophies of transcendentalism and yoga, for most of us simple methods
of relaxing the mind will have to be enough. One such method was taught

to me by Mr Wu. I had learned in lectures at Chin Wu that meditation had played a vital part in the lives of great masters of the past. Only the simplest and most basic forms were taught to the novice, to be developed within his own capacity until years of practice brought their own reward. I visited Mr Wu unexpectedly one evening. He was not in the pool or on the terrace and his servant seemed unwilling to tell me where he was. For a moment I was afraid I had walked in on one of those rare occasions when he entertained a lady at home.

The servant bowed me to my usual chair and would have left to fix me a calamansi had I not insisted on knowing the whereabouts of his master. 'He is thinking, sir. You must find him quietly.' He pointed to a far corner of the garden which I had always believed to be a dense thicket of bamboo.

I found a cave-like opening in the ivory-smooth trunks. They creaked like the masts of a ship. The carpet of leaves made it possible to approach softly and the rustling all around deadened any noise I may have made. In the middle of the thicket was a clearing, in the centre of the clearing a small pool fed by a primitive tip-up fountain of the type found in Japanese monasteries. I saw the flash of carp in the pool, lit by the shards of moonlight that found their way into this hidden glade. They also lit a small shrine which the silent water surrounded. The air was heavy with incense from the cherry red sparks of joss sticks that pricked the dark before the shrine.

'Sit. I will tell you a poem and show you how to think about it.'

The quiet voice of Mr Wu came from the shadows. He sat naked to the waist, in the half lotus position, straight-backed and with the right hand resting in the left palm. His head was erect and facing the flowering joss, their tiny glow tinting the shrine. I copied his position and waited.

'You must concentrate on the burning tip of the joss through half-closed eyes. Clear your mind of all else but the depths. Listen to these words and try to memorise them. Think of nothing else. The words are from the Tao.'

"Close your eyes and you will see clearly.
Cease to listen and you will hear truth.
Be silent and your heart will sing.
Seek no contacts and you will find union.
Be still and you will move forward on the tide of spirit.
Be gentle and you will need no strength.
Be patient and you will achieve all things.
Be humble and you will remain entire."

In time I did memorise the words and forced myself to reflect on them. I learned to meditate to the best of my ability but soon I found my mind insisted on going its own way. The Taoist poem was meaningful but I had not been there. It was someone else's haven. I found that my basic concept of meditation was a sort of return to childhood. I had havens of my own. Most of us will admit that our appreciation of beautiful things, our absolute delight with the gifts of nature, has never been as clear-cut, as simply enchanting as when we were tiny. Perhaps it was because we knew so little and expected less. Can we remember our first serious contemplation of dew, those silver beads, strung diamond-brilliant along the network of a cobweb, the world reflected on a grass-tip or cradled by a leaf? Have flowers been as carefully scrutinised, their scents as openly breathed since then? Haven't trees lost a little of their majesty and skies become a little smaller? Are animals

and insects half as friendly?

Even the harshest childhood had its vital moments, its magnificent discoveries, never to be re-captured but only to be looked back on as dreams. For me there were two such 'secrets'. They were places, sanctuaries known only to me. One was in the great, rough arms of a giant elm, access gained by barked shins, grazed knees and no little risk of breaking my neck. Above, the wind-ruffled intricacy of leaves and birds, the darting light was like a cut-glass chandelier. The safe smell of moss and fungus, out of reach from everyone but God, whom I fervently believed was somewhere in that tree.

The other was in a field adjoining the school, which I was too young to attend. In summer its breezy grasses were uncut because no haymaker seemed to own it. Only the brewer's dray horse, great, brown and alone, stayed close to its hedges and explored it with his teeth. I found a spot where the cow parsley grew to the height of trees and the thick green clumps of dock leaves served as skating rinks for snails. There was an alder against an old brick wall and old, red dust came off when I leaned against it. I made a hiding place there, flattening the grass the way an animal does by turning round and round before lying down. From it I could watch the world, unseen except for clouds that moved over the wall and the sweet-scented wall-flowers that blew on top of it, with a lark above them. I shared that sacred spot with green-backed grasshoppers, scarlet ladybirds and a family of blackbirds that argued in the alder.

I was probably four years old at the time and yet I have learned to revisit those exclusive places of mine, almost fifty years later. I can quite easily recall the rustle of the leaves that seemed to separate the sky, the piping of a visiting thrush and the smell of moss and fungus close to my cheek. It is not hard, if I concentrate, to clearly breathe the unmistakable perfume of red and yellow wall-flowers and hear grasshoppers shrilling all around me.

I choose those places to meditate because I am sure I was nearest to myself and to my Maker when I was there. Think back, if you intend to meditate, as far as you can go. Find the time and place where life was best and your world at its simplest, and begin again for those few moments.

An hour or two before retiring, go to the place of your choice. If it is in the spot where you practise Pa Tuan Tsin, so much the better. Set a lighted joss stick or candle in a small jar or other suitable container on the floor and turn out the light. Sit in the half lotus position, straighten the back and remain as erect as possible. Place the back of the relaxed right hand into the cupped palm of the relaxed left hand (like a swallow in its nest.) Half close the eyes and concentrate intensely upon the red spark before you. Transfer any unwanted thoughts to the spark which for these moments has become your universe.

If the mind refuses to empty itself, recite the words of the poem (or any other which for you may have a pleasant meaning) and concentrate on your chosen time and place until a single element, a sight or sound or scent, perhaps all three, is floating there inside the flame. The essence of peace. Hold it there for five to fifteen minutes. If at first discomfort makes it difficult to remain perfectly still, try to ignore it: one aspect of meditation is endurance. If you can ignore pain for some seconds it will begin to be of less importance . . . eventually it will cease to exist.

The ultimate meditation is a trance-like state which leads to the ultimate control of bodily sensations. It is why the shaman, the fakir or the yogi can pierce his own flesh without reaction and endure days, months or years of intense privation without a murmur.

Extend the period of meditation as you feel inclined, do not force yourself past a stage which commonsense warns is enough. Let it come slowly and do not expect it to come at all.

> 'Sweet is solitude and peace of mind.
> Sweet is to be free from fear or desire.
> Hold fast to the truth as your refuge.'
>
> Gautama Buddha

PART NINE

THE POWER OF CHI

'The three walks of life:
to walk in the heavens,
to walk on the water,
but first to walk the way of the Tao'
Lin Tui

The Power of Chi

Reading back through these pages, I have tried to see if I have missed anything of importance to someone who is ready to begin improving his or her health through Pa Tuan Tsin. There are one or two points worth mentioning and a couple worth repeating.

I think the most important subject, which perhaps has not emerged as strongly as it should, is that of mental attitude. Firstly, admit that you are not as well as you could be and that unless you do something about it not only will you get no better, but eventually you will get worse. Secondly, it is important to be more than moderately interested in what you have read and more than tentative about trying it out. You should be utterly convinced by it and find the determination to practise it with the patience and fortitude any such intrusive procedure initially demands.

Since the message of this book is primarily aimed at people for whom, either through illness or advancing age, the bloom of youth has passed, this closing chapter is addressed to them in particular.

I wish I could have been even more persuasive, or found some unique way of making certain that you practise what I have suggested as religiously as I did for at least a month. If you were to do that I know you would continue until these exercises become as much a comforting part of your life as they are of mine. You will have experienced, whatever age you have reached, the wonderful changes that improved health can bring about through the simple process of concentrating on your breathing for a given period each day. You will have taken this blessing from the air around you. Air, Chi, Prana, Ki, intrinsic energy, life force, call it what you will, it is yours by right . . . the first thing given to you on this earth and the last thing to be taken away.

Improving your health, the quality of your life and your attitude towards it, brings not only renewed confidence in yourself and your own capabilities, but a fresh confidence in life itself. The things that you find difficult to cope with at home or at work, the innermost worries that are yours and no one else's, even the people you prefer to avoid, will be more easily faced and overcome.

What then are the sorts of attitudes that may prevent you from taking full advantage of Pa Tuan Tsin? One is the fact that you may be fully aware of the need for exercise and already engaged in a full routine. 'Hold on,' you might say, 'I happen to play squash three times a week, golf on Sundays, run most mornings. What more can I do?'

Well, if this is the case, whatever you are doing it obviously isn't enough or you would not have picked up this book. Any exercise is good but very few routines are benefiting us all-round, that is to say, as good for all of the inside as it is for all of the outside. As we have said, the Western concept of exercise tends to be cosmetic. As long as we develop good muscles, retain our shape and keep our waist as slim as we can, we look great and all is well.

We have made it very easy for ourselves to keep in good shape with every facility within easy reach of anyone with the need and energy to use it. We are constantly reminded of just how easy it is to keep looking well. If we don't have a swimming pool or tennis courts in our garden there are bound to be some within easy reach. We are constantly reminded of keep-fit programmes that go hand in hand with certain breakfast cereals, easily practised in the privacy of our own room for as little as three minutes and a few cents a day. Television commercials, print ads and radio jingles offer us equipment we can buy or hire to row, pedal, push or pull towards a body like the one in the advertisement. We can have our hair dyed or even transplanted, our teeth capped, breasts inflated, noses changed, wrinkles removed, faces lifted and flesh shifted or carved off. There is nothing we cannot and will not do about our *outward* appearance while most of us let the *inside* upon which everything else depends, take care of itself and do very little to encourage it.

The Chinese, on the other hand (and many Asians, for that matter), consider the outward appearance of little importance compared to the inner condition. They have a saying which, loosely translated, means: 'It is useless to look forty when you are fifty, if inside you are sixty'. They also feel strongly about over- exercising certain parts of the body while neglecting other parts. As always, they have a saying: 'The legs of a bull will not get far on the heart of a chicken'. Or, 'A powerful arm does nothing for a weak stomach'.

'The world has always been quoting such fortune cookie philosophies,' you say, 'but what does it mean?' Well, it is true that in recent years Western medical science has taken another look at certain aspects of our physical culture. For instance, they have found that jogging for people of certain age, weight and condition can do far more harm than good, particularly jogging on concrete, which has a jarring effect on the spine and may have serious repercussions in later years. The rigours of the weight-lifting gym can do more harm than good unless carefully overseen. Even the beneficial rays of the sun have come under increasing scrutiny with the realisation that indiscriminate sunbathing when young not only ages skin long before its time, but may well result in skin disease and even cancer later on. On the other hand, health programmes, exercise methods, preventive medicine, mythical cures from the Orient, and so on, are getting more and more attention from occidental experts. 'Acupuncture, moxibustion, herb remedies, youth drugs, love philtres and massage, are age-old healing methods that astound modern medical science', was one remark made by leading American surgeon, Dr Samuel Rosen, on his return from China in 1970. He had been invited to witness acupuncture and other practices of Chinese folk medicine. He summed up for the *New York Times* as follows: 'I have seen the past and it works'.

We of the West stretch our imaginations when we contemplate the 'Bionic Man' . . . a futuristic possibility which will no doubt one day result in a half man, half machine. Yet for thousands of years strict followers of Yoga, Zen, other Asian and some African cults have been able to influence such functions as pulse rate, breathing, digestion, sexual control, metabolism and kidney activity at will. They can slow the heartbeat to what would normally be lethal levels, reduce their respiration to one breath every few minutes and suspend the life force to enable themselves to be buried alive for days. They have total control of the reflexes that cause the normal man to avoid intense pain and can divert them at will, allowing spikes and blades to pierce their flesh without causing the slightest reaction, even controlling the flow of blood.

Why should we disbelieve, then, astounding claims of longevity or question such feats as those accomplished by the 'mountain leapers' of Tibet. These monks who live in rugged and almost inaccessible upland wastes long ago produced their own version of bionic man. By practising the art of Lung-gom they are able to cover the ground in great leaps and bounds, bouncing from one spot to the next with the elasticity of an India rubber ball. They have been known to cover a distance of 480 kilometres between sunrise of one day and midday of the next, travelling at a speed of 16 kilometres per hour over very inhospitable terrain. The West's great marathon runners average 19 kilometres per hour on good roads for a maximum of two hours at a stretch.

Another classic example is the Tibetan practice of Tumo, the art of bearing the cold. Through a highly complex system of breathing exercises and meditation these hermits are able to live high up in the regions of permanent snow and go about completely naked or in nothing but a thin cotton garment. The test of a novice would be enough to kill any normal human being: after months of bathing in icy streams and sitting naked in the snow, he is wrapped in a sheet which has been dipped through a hole in the ice of a lake, and left to sit outside all night. The sheet must be completely dried by his body heat and replaced by a wet one at least three times before sunrise.

Of course, such superhuman accomplishments don't come easily. A lifetime of self-discipline leads to an ordeal such as the training for Lung-gom, where the initiate must sit in complete darkness and seclusion for thirty-nine months, all the while performing deep-breathing exercises. Is such dedication to developing the human body, mind and soul to such limits any less valuable than spending billions to build a false one?

The Air We Breathe

A question I am often asked, and something about which you may be wondering, is what of the quality of air? 'What use is it,' you could ask, 'for me to apply myself to this business of breathing properly when I live in a city where the air is so foul I would be wiser breathing as little of it as possible?' We have lived with pollution and its ever-present threats for too long not to be aware of the difference between good and bad air. Of course, one who daily breathes the untainted air of high altitudes, of the open countryside or of the sea, is more fortunate than one who has to make the best of city smog. It even 'tastes' better.

Fortunately, nature has equipped every one of us with a built-in filtering and refining system which, provided we use it properly, renders even the worst air breathable, as long as there is sufficient oxygen present. What is meant by using it properly? The answer is simple. By *always* inhaling through the nose and *never* inhaling through the mouth. Again, the Chinese have a saying: 'Only a fool will stuff food up his nose. To take air through the mouth is no better.' Not as absurd as it sounds, it simply demonstrates that the nostrils are intended for breathing and the mouth is intended for eating.

A more recent, and perhaps more practical, illustration is found in 'The Good Health Battle Plan' by Dr Donald Norfolk, published in the June 1978 issue of *Cosmopolitan* magazine.

'One habit to be avoided is mouth-breathing. When we breathe through the nose, we warm and filter the inspired air. It has been estimated that we inhale 20 billion particles of foreign matter a day. When we breathe through the nose, most of these bits of dirt and dust are trapped in the sticky mucus that lines the airways. From there they are wafted harmlessly to the stomach by the cilia, the fine hairs that exert a constant sweeping action over the surface of the mucus membranes. Experimental animals have been given dirty air to breathe at temperatures ranging from 500°C to minus 100°C and in every case, the air was cleaned and warmed to body temperature before it entered the lungs. Such is the efficiency of the body's air-conditioning apparatus, providing it is not by-passed by breathing through the mouth. A further advantage of breathing through the nose is that it helps clear the sinuses.'

The other thing we can do to make the most of our share of oxygen is to let it in, not shut it out. Ventilation is as sensible as breathing through the apparatus we have been given for the purpose. We know that if we shut ourselves in a confined space for long enough, we will use up the oxygen and continually recycle the air until it becomes nothing but waste, as used up and useless as any other of the body's waste matters.

For those who live in cold climates the houses, places of work and, particularly, bedrooms, are too often tightly sealed, for the sake of our health. We are led to believe that cold is bad for us and that exposure to it can lead to colds, 'flu and other serious bronchial and respiratory illnesses. Of course, it can if we allow the temperature to drop too low, or wear inadequate clothing and have insufficient covering on our beds. But we were meant to live with cold, and living with it intelligently is not difficult.

The same, applies to those who live in the tropics. Air-conditioning, which depends on sealed space for efficiency, is a poor alternative to fresh air, no matter how high its temperature. The problem of keeping cool is generally greater for Western people living in Eastern climates. No matter how long a European lives in an equatorial or excessively hot country, he or she will find it almost impossible to survive comfortably without air-conditioning. In the days of the Raj, in the furnace heat of India, the sahibs and memsahibs turned to punkah fans and hill stations for relief. Now we pay mightily for fully air-conditioned hotels, accommodation and offices while the natives of that country continue to work and play in the conditions they were born to thrive in.

The air we breathe is made up of positive (destructive) ions, and negative (energy-giving) ions. The less oxygen or pure air in our surroundings the more prevalent the positive ions; the more oxygen or pure air in our surroundings the more prevalent the negative ions. That is to say, the rarefied air of a mountain top, the middle of a forest or a field, with its oxygen-making foliage and plant life, or the ozone of an ocean, would be predominantly made up of life-giving negative ions. The further we get away from these natural ideals and the closer to man-made cities, with their industrial complexes, traffic and lack of greenery, the more laden the air becomes with unhealthy positive ions.

The problem is considered serious by many scientists. The study of biometeorology, which has been taking place since the 1930s, is of major importance in such countries as Switzerland, East Germany and Hungary, and is best summed up in *The Ion Effect* (Fred Soyka and Alan Edmonds, Bantam, New York, 1978). Mr Soyka, who spent many years researching his subject throughout the world, explains how air electricity rules our lives and health. He analyses the adverse effects of those bizarre climatic conditions kown as the 'Witches' Winds'; the Föhn of the European Alps; Italy's sirocco; the Santa Anna in California, known to the Indians as the 'Bitter Winds', which blows from the deserts of northern Arizona down into Mexico; the Chinook of Western Canada and the United States; the Sharav (or Hamsin) of Israel and the Middle East; and the sinister Mistral of southern France. All of these winds have strange and disquieting effects upon those in their path. Suicide rates soar, traffic accidents become almost epidemic and, at best, we feel a little 'under the weather' or 'out of sorts'.

The significant thing about these observations seems to be that the air during these winds is found to be predominantly charged with positive ions and very low on negative ions, similar to the man-made conditions we have created in our cities and modern buildings through air-conditioning and central heating — not to mention the pollution of transportation and industry.

These discoveries have led some of the world's most eminent scientists to turn their attention to the development of ionisation. Dr Albert P. Krueger, Emeritus Professor of Bacteriology at the University of California, and Israel's Dr Felix Gad Sulman have put up a case so convincing that the World Health Organisation and World Meteorological Organisation have co-operated in drawing such environmental dangers to the notice of architects and town planners, car and aircraft designers, and others who create the man-made environments that most of us are forced to live with.

Russia and the nations of Eastern Europe are far more advanced in biometeorology than the nations of the West, with the exception of Switzerland. In these countries ionisers are a part of standard hospital equipment in operating theatres, post-operative recovery wards, delivery rooms and intensive care units. (Ionisers are electronic units that emit negative ions.)

By 1975 an East German doctor had treated more than 11 000 patients with 'neg-ion' therapy. They responded, he said, with monotonous regularity. Brazilian hospitals have long been using ion generators and Switzerland's Dr Russell Stark initiated its use in factories and office complexes with a dramatic improvement in staff performance.

The Power of Chi

I suppose the most pointed, and certainly the most frequent, question I am asked in relation to my faith in the cultivation of Chi is 'What makes you so positive about the effects of these breathing exercises? Surely any form of exercise, considering the fact that you were out of condition at the time, would have made you look and feel better. Do you really think it is worth putting into a book?'

Perhaps then, this is the best question with which to conclude.

My belief in the power of Chi or, to sound less dramatic, the absolute importance of developing any degree of inner strength through breath control, was, of course, given to me by personal acquaintance with the Chin Wu School. In the early stages I was impressed and awed by the everyday displays of sheer physical excellence that I saw there. Then this astonishment grew into genuine interest and complete enthusiasm. The infinite patience and flawless example of remarkable people like Mr Wu, Master Chan, Johnny Chuetin, the White Crane champion I have called 'D' and so many other students and instructors of Wu Shu cannot fail to persuade even the most stubborn cynic. To witness and become even a small part of such power coupled with humility is in itself a revelation. But I also think it was the sheer common sense of Chin Wu philosophy, the practical concept of breathing for health that convinced me and provided the discipline.

I considered my own background. I remembered how, when physical effort had been my way of life, I had relied on the ability to breathe properly as a matter of course; I used breath as a tool to not only accomplish manual labour but to actually enjoy it. I remembered that it would have been impossible to fell a tree without breathing being an integral part of bodily rhythm; to try to swing an axe or a hammer all day without the measured lung power to drive home force would be futile.

I then realised, with a measure of shock, that since I had given up the physical, outdoor life and begun the long climb to respectability, responsibility and 'success', I had also given up the ability to breathe. It came to me that in almost a quarter of a century I had forgotten what real breathing was like. I reflected upon the years of sitting behind a desk, the wheel of a car, in an easy chair before a television screen, never conscious of my breath unless I was forced to use it, and only to find myself 'out of it' in a matter of minutes.

Although I have tried to pass on as effectively as possible the way I feel about breathing for health, I fully realise that the personal experiences and convictions of one person are rarely enough to motivate another. Nevertheless, it may be worth relating what is perhaps the closest to tangible proof of the power of Chi.

Although I had fallen into the trap of 'good living' and experiencing the gradual physical decline that so often goes with it, I had never been really ill. I had not seen the inside of a hospital and seldom called upon a doctor, even at the age of forty-five. I had all my own teeth, a good head of hair and had always been strong, due perhaps to so many years of healthy physical work in my younger days. But, although I had survived the stresses and strains of a 'busy' life as best I could, it had left me a fairly heavy drinker and an even heavier smoker. Only when my stamina was suddenly tried did it occur to me that I had been deceiving myself for a long time.

Then in March 1975, whilst living in the Philippines, I began to loose my voice. I put it down to the epidemic of laryngitis that was going around Manila at the time and, apart from inhaling various concoctions and resting my voice when possible, I waited without too much concern for it to pass.

I was nearing the end of my first year with Chin Wu and on one particular evening I had been called upon to lead the class through the warm-up exercises and Pa Tuan Tsin. It was customary to count loudly for each set of movements and when my voice failed completely in the middle of a set Master C called a replacement and led me into his little office.

'Have you seen a doctor about your throat?' he asked, casually. I nodded. 'What does he say?' 'Laryngitis,' I croaked. 'Would you come to see a Chinese doctor?' His tone was so serious and his eyes so steady that I quickly agreed.

The little man he took me to could have been a grocer or a retired gardener. Instead, he was one of the most famous traditional Chinese doctors in the Philippines. He sat me down and looked me over almost nonchalantly, as though appraising my clothes. Without a word, he left the small table that served as his desk and stood before me. 'Take off your shoes and shirt and breath quietly,' he said, and he put his fingertips very lightly on the soles of my feet, my ankles, my underarms and my neck and throat. At each point of contact he paused for up to ten or twenty seconds, his eyes closed and raised to the ceiling. In less than a minute he had finished his examination and, after a short discussion with Master C., he bowed us out.

'He says you have a growth on the larynx," Master C. said briskly as soon as we were outside. 'He says you must tell your doctor to check you into the hospital for a biopsy without delay. It has been with you for months."

The shock of a positive cancer test is probably one of the most severe emotions one can face. It is an overwhelming feeling of lonely despair coupled with a little flame of hope that usually flickers until it is put out. A feeling of having been singled out and punished. But it is not really something one can attempt to describe to another, so I will try no further. It is enough to say that in little more than forty-eight hours I was being fitted for my radiation mask in the Radiotherapy Unit of Hammersmith Hospital, just outside central London. The experiences and emotions that one goes through while undergoing radiotherapy is a subject that would fill another book and is certainly not necessary here. What is relevant is the way in which Pa Tuan Tsin helped me through five consecutive weeks of maximum super-voltage, its effect on the results of the treatment and the vital part it played in my rehabilitation.

A BBC interviewer recently asked me a rather obvious if not well thought out question. 'If,' said the confident lady, 'you were already a regular practitioner of the respiratory exercise routine you so enthusiastically recommend, when you detected so classic a respiratory disease did it not cast a little doubt upon the preventive powers the exercises are claimed to offer?'

It had of course, crossed my mind, until the Director of Radiotherapy, and one of Britain's leading specialists, explained that science can not detect when, why or where malignant cells first develop. In respiratory cancer (throat and lungs) it is firmly believed that heavy smoking, together with poor respiratory function considerably increases the grim prospect, but is not necessarily its root cause. Some people, he explained, may have given up smoking for years and still suffer from the disease, the seeds of which can have been sown up to twenty years earlier. Once there and once activated it must be fought with all the power of the universe and the mortal soul. The BBC lady seemed little impressed by this answer, as she mashed out another half-smoked Salem among the thirty or forty already in the ashtray beside her.

The first days of treatment are briefly described in my diary:
'The Vicarage. May 16th. 6.30am.

We are staying the weekend at the Vicarage. It is in a lovely old place about thirty minutes from Waterloo. This lovely part, which is on a green, slow-flowing river hidden by willows has become a little hemmed-in by housing estates, but there are some things they cannot ruin and this river is one of them. Tomorrow is my first day of treatment. My first dose of radiation, then there are only twenty-nine to go. The doc says thirty doses are as far as they can go without risk of permanent damage. My mask is finished and fits like a skin. The planning is done and the calculations that will direct the beam have been checked and rechecked and entered in a thin record book with my name on it. Tomorrow the fight begins. I think of all the times I have complained and all the times I have almost given up. And I tell you, God, I am ashamed. The water of that river is calm and deep. Its current is sluggish and ripples round the stems of lilies. Dragonflies patrol the clumps of reeds and a family of ducks wades among them to head upstream. It is dawn and I have come here to take my breathing exercises and practise the dance of the Mantis. I tried doing it in the Vicarage garden but the sight of it alarmed the neighbours. I wonder how the Shaolin monks handled cancer.

St. James Park. May 17th. 6am.

The first morning of my treatment begins as bravely as a warrior preparing for combat. I jog to St James Park to single out my favourite tree. It is 6am and grey, as I bounce past faces black, brown, cream and yellow. I feel like waving to the pink ones. Past the thronging bus stops, crowds poised at pedestrian crossings like United Nations assault troops waiting for a signal. I want to wave to them all. "Mornin' all . . . 'ave a nice day, we're all English now . . . it's us against the rest." They seem to know I'm a stranger. Skipping over a dog poop, nimble as a forty-seven year old gnome. I want to shout at them. "I belong here y'know. Born and bred. In uniform at fourteen, me. I've got a right to be here. This is my country." The faces don't encourage such frivolity.

In the park, among exploding buds and under spreads of new green, a golden ash vibrating in the breeze; gleaming chestnut flanks trot and canter along the bridle paths. Immaculate riders, some uniformed in the regimental blue of Guards, others sport the tailored habit and hard hat of the very rich. A tramp rolls from under a shelter of dew-damp deck chairs; they are propped against a fallen elm . . . the elm had taken a century or two to grow, now its heart is eaten out with elm blight all the way from Holland. The tramp adjusts the newspaper beneath his coat, much as a passing lady rider adjusts her silken cravat, and settles down to watch me approach the bottom of my imaginary mountain.

The radiation tank. May 18th.

Half a ton of lead shifts aside like a Churchill tank cranking its turret onto a feeble target. I feel like a grain of sand, singled out from a desert. All the power of the universe is aimed at my throat. That great clunk, the nippy little nurse had told me before retreating in her soft white shoes, was the lead shielding sliding aside, to let the weasel see the rabbit. I resented her. Untouchable in her neat early morning white, smelling of starch and Lifebuoy as she bends close to bolt the protective shield in place, warm breath, faintly Pepsodent. Where's the mumsy one with her "cuppa and a Woodbine" manner?

"Try not to swallow and whatever happens don't move." Move? How can I move? With this thing holding me from chin to chest like a vice. I feel like Frankenstein's dangerous puppet. My eyes swivel to the Mobiltron poised above me, big as a searchlight. The Mobiltron, invention of the great and humane, clanked around on its giant crane arm. Tiny window in its middle winking like a cyclops eye, fine, crossed hairs sighting its centre. Power of a thousand suns. That's what the Japs had said when the Yanks dropped it on Hiroshima. Baked thousands of people in their tracks and scorched the world. Now here it was, tame as a working elephant. Trundling obediently on its chain around this giant's quadrant to try and save another life.

"You won't feel anything," she had said as she adjusted the wedge under my arched neck. "Just a sort of thump as the lead drops then a faint buzzing." She smiled briefly as a blink. "Larynx is easy to get at. Only two minutes each side. Try to think of something else". I thought of my spot under the alder and the sound of flies buzzing on the wall, a ladybird climbing a stalk of grass. And the buzz of the Mobiltron became a bright green grasshopper rubbing its back legs together."

Throughout the five weeks of super-voltage radiation, the early morning practise of Pa Tuan Tsin was not only a great source of physical and mental well-being but it produced tangible and somewhat amazing results. Exposure to intense radiation is expected to have its negative side-effects, and each patient is given a little book to warn and prepare them for what is to come. Weight loss, loss of appetite, loss of sleep and a general downturn in spirit are the most typical. I am glad to say that at no time did I experience any of these. I slept soundly without sedatives, ate ravenously, drank my quota of draught Guinness at the 'local' each evening and maintained a steady certainty about the outcome.

Even case-hardened doctors and nurses were impressed and asked me to demonstrate the Precious Set Of Eight. It was their interest and obvious understanding of the importance of respiratory exercise that prompted me to write and publish what had been given to me.

Before leaving you to decide whether you will add this book to those on the shelf to be dusted once a week, or whether you will open it each morning and begin improving your health, there is one brief point I feel I must repeat. While compiling this material, I have tussled with the nagging concern that, in spite of my efforts to explain to the contrary, the result may be misinterpreted as an attempt to teach or preach some facets of the martial arts. I feel I must, for the last time, emphasise that it is not. In presenting a little of the history of Wu Shu and mentioning a few of its past and present champions, I have merely tried to provide a background to the exercises that are the book's only purpose. It only represents that which I have learned and used to my great benefit from the Chin Wu Athletic Association of the Philippines, those connected with it, and in particular Master Shakespeare Chan who gave me permission to pass it on in this way.

Any serious student of Wu Shu or any other form of martial art would probably consider it the ABC of their craft. Although they may not have been fully aware of the ancient Shaolin ritual of Pa Tuan Tsin they would certainly have grounded their training on some similar routine of breathing exercises, and may consider it tame reading indeed. One cannot be involved in Wu Shu without being humbly aware of the tremendous physical, mental and material demands made upon the genuine follower who hopes for a recognised place in this exceptional society. The rigid discipline of self-denial throughout the better part of a lifetime, the personal courage and individual conquest set him aside from the ordinary.

Those who would like to know more about the ancient art of Chinese

Temple Boxing, those perhaps who find that the practice of Pa Tuan Tsin leads them further, will find what they need in Master Chee Soo's remarkable book '*A Step by Step Guide to Kung Fu*' (Promotional Printing Ltd, London, 1975) or they may contact the International Wu Shu Association, 90 Albanks, Dunstable, Bedfordshire, England. Complete information on all aspects of Asian health cultures may be found in *Oriental Methods of Mental and Physical Fitness* by Dr Pierre Huard and Ming Wong (Funk and Wagnall, New York, 1920).

It seems I have said all that I can about the importance of improved breathing and cultivation of the vital Chi through the Eight Precious Sets of Exercises. Even if they do not become a regular part of your daily life you may at least have faced the shape you are in and realised that any improvement in your breathing habits can only help you to live and love longer through the power of Chi. Proof? The real proof is within you. Only your own efforts and their results will prove to be of any real meaning or benefit to you: your own patience and your own fortitude. This book can only show you the foot of the mountain, it cannot make you climb.

For me, the opportunity came later in my life than I would have liked and at a time when total dedication to the demands and disciplines were both impractical and impossible. It may well be the same for you. I have satisfied myself with knowledge enough to pass on in the interests of improved health and am grateful to my teachers and friends in the Brotherhood for the opportunity. The intricacies and refinements to be found further up the mountain I leave to those who have earned the right to teach it.

It is up to you how far you go or whether you turn back before you begin. It's your life, your spirit, your body and your health. Master Chee Soo sums it up with a saying passed on by his Master, Chan Lee:

"A reflection in a pool never reveals its depth. To know that, you must enter the water."

So, get your feet wet. The yogis of old were right: in this competitive and demanding age, keeping fit and able is not just a fad, it is a duty. A duty to yourself, the one that gave you life and those who depend upon you to remain strong. Stop relying on those inadequate little breaths and start learning to fill your lungs the way you were intended to. Start breathing for your life and love. And when you have found what it can do for you, teach it to others so that we can all live longer and love longer through the power of Chi.